GLASSBLOWING
A Search for Form

GLASSBLOWING

A Search for Form Harvey K. Littleton

VNR VAN NOSTRAND REINHOLD COMPANY

New York Cincinnati Toronto London Melbourne

To my wife Bess
without whose harrassment and challenge
this book would not be possible

Van Nostrand Reinhold Company Regional Offices:
New York   Cincinnati   Chicago   Millbrae   Dallas

Van Nostrand Reinhold Company International Offices:
London   Toronto   Melbourne

Copyright © 1971 by Litton Educational Publishing, Inc.
Library of Congress Catalog Card Number 73-153458

Designed by Jean Callan King

Type set by Cooper & Beatty, Limited, Toronto, Canada
Printed by Halliday Lithograph Corporation
Color printed by Il Resto del Carlino, Bologna, Italy
Bound by Publishers Book Bindery, Inc.

Published by Van Nostrand Reinhold Company
450 West 33rd Street, New York, N.Y. 10001

Published simultaneously in Canada by
Van Nostrand Reinhold Ltd.

16 15 14 13 12 11 10 9 8 7 6 5 4 3 2 1

CONTENTS

Preface

A search for form is the daily pursuit of the artist. The search until recently somehow overlooked the blowing of molten glass directly from the furnace.

There has long been popular confusion about even the term "glassblowing," which has been used to mean, as we do in this book, work with the blowpipe using molten glass from the furnace, as well as the traditional use of rods and tubes of glass manipulated in a flame, mainly for the production of scientific glassware.

In Corning, my birthplace, there was always great rivalry and little love between the masters of both crafts. The gaffer, the head of the team blowing glass from the furnace, stood very high in the esteem of the town. He wore a white shirt to work, was absolute dictator in his area of the factory, and received the highest pay. The lampworkers, as the others were called, were also highly skilled and well paid, and they worked alone. In addition, they often had a bench fixed up at home for production of swans, swizzle sticks, and full-rigged ships—novelties they could give as gifts or sell. Gaffers and would-be gaffers also worked when they could to make their traditional gifts and objects for sale or barter. Colored canes and glass chains and paperweights were favorites. Some of these were traded to saloonkeepers for drinks, as the best gaffers were also the best drinkers.

The rivalry between the two types of glassworker has contributed to the confusion in terms. In the title of his book, *Flameworking: Glassmaking for the Craftsman,* Frederic Schuler has used a new term. Flameworking is more descriptive of the activity of the lampworker and a much more accurate name, as the source of heat for such work is no longer the alcohol lamp of the early nineteenth century; lampworkers now use more sophisticated torches which burn gas-oxygen mixtures.

Glass, an endlessly intriguing material, remains virtually undiscovered as a medium for artistic expression despite the millions of dollars lavished on its manufacture and the diversification of products in glass. My book is both a guide and a revivalist manifesto. In particular, the book describes the way hand-blown articles are made from molten glass, explains why artists in increasing numbers choose to work in this rather primitive way, encourages other artists to try the same thing, and still others who may not be artists to appreciate and collect the articles that are created. It is my purpose to suggest the dimensions of glass as a medium for the artist, rather than to define its properties or to set rules and limits for its formation. The book is inevitably a statement of my own motivations, sources, and concepts, which I hope will provide a base for growth—for myself, my students, other practitioners, critics, collectors, and the others who love glass. Ours is a small segment of the art world, and an even smaller segment of the world of glass, but I believe it to be exciting and important to both.

The complete coverage of the composition of glass and its nature, the materials, tools, and techniques of forming, furnace design, and finishing can be found in the technical literature and in industry, and it is expanding continually. The complete catalog of past achievements can be found in libraries and museums. But there is no guide or introduction to these technical and aesthetic works to give an artist any point of reference. The very richness of the historical background and the breadth of technical achievement today point the way toward a tremendous future for glass as a vehicle for the artist. That it has escaped his notice until now is something of a mystery.

Opposite, works by the author—
Top left:
BLOWN FORM, 1962

Bottom left:
AMETHYST VASE, 1962.

Right:
"TRIUMPH," ALUMINUM AND CRYSTAL
GLASS CORD WITH COPPER BLUE, 1970.

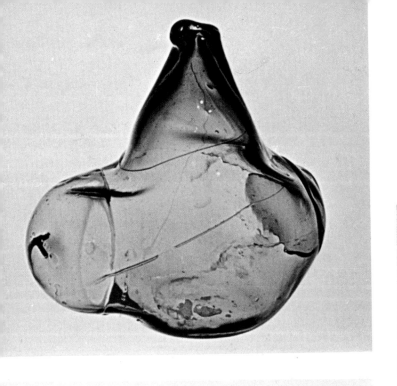

An intimate working knowledge of many materials is characteristic of the modern artist, especially in America. The graduates of the modern art schools are equally at home working with wood, steel, bronze, plastics, canvas and paper, hand tools and power tools; and the search for new materials and techniques is not only a part of the scene but may even be one of the driving forces. The adventurous spirit of artists today has led them to tackle and master techniques heretofore thought to be solely within the province of industry, techniques such as electroforming, vacuum forming, iron founding, photo- and electrostatic printing, and a myriad of others. Glass, with its unique hot-working properties and its depth, brilliant color, and optical effects, is naturally an intriguing challenge.

Such investigations have occurred within the framework of the revolution in the arts in America since World War II. This revolution began with the Abstract Expressionists. A great number of mature young men, veterans of the war, swelled the graduate art classes and assaulted the various media with the same determination they had used in France and in the South Pacific. The directness and spontaneity of action painting was quickly felt in sculpture, pottery, metal, weaving, and printmaking.

Many of us involved in pottery were greatly excited as the forms in our medium began to change from the traditional teapots, bowls, and vases to become huge forms of torn and beaten clay. We utilized all the skills and knowledge of our craft and borrowed from industry and improvised new techniques to make the new forms possible. The acceptance of the work of potters like Peter Voulkos, John Mason, and David Weinrib in the large sculpture exhibitions at the Whitney Museum, The Art Institute of Chicago, and elsewhere greatly expanded the horizons for all of us. With the advent of neo-Dada—Pop Art—the potters started producing clay soft-drink bottles, toilets, typewriters, ceramic shoes, and later, as many turned to bronze, brooms, and paper bags in metal. Today many are equally concerned with optical—Op—art and minimal art.

It was during this proliferation of forms and directions, this art explosion, that glass was introduced into the university art curriculum on the graduate level in September 1962 at the University of Wisconsin. There are now, in 1971, over fifty American colleges, universities, and schools offering glass as another medium for young artists to explore.

Although trained as a potter and an industrial designer, I never forgot my early infatuation with glass, which began with childhood visits to my father's laboratory in the Corning Glass Works and continued through two summers' work at Corning when I was in college. I taught and worked as a potter at Toledo and the University of Wisconsin and did not get back to glass until by chance I was asked to do some research for Corning during a projected trip to Europe in 1957. When I was in New York to discuss my commission, I asked Arthur Houghton if he knew of any glassworkers who worked alone as artists. He mentioned Jean Sala in Paris. I visited Sala, and when I told him of my interest in glass he found some old tools to give me and sent me on my way.

The American Crafts Council, through its conference in 1959 at Lake George, raised the question of the possibility of glass—especially blown glass—as a medium for the artist. I took upon myself the challenge to try to develop the techniques necessary for a person to work alone as an artist in glass. In 1961, at the next conference, I was able to report some progress, and the following year to interest

GLASS PIECES CARVED FROM LUMPS OF CULLET
BY THE AUTHOR, 1960.

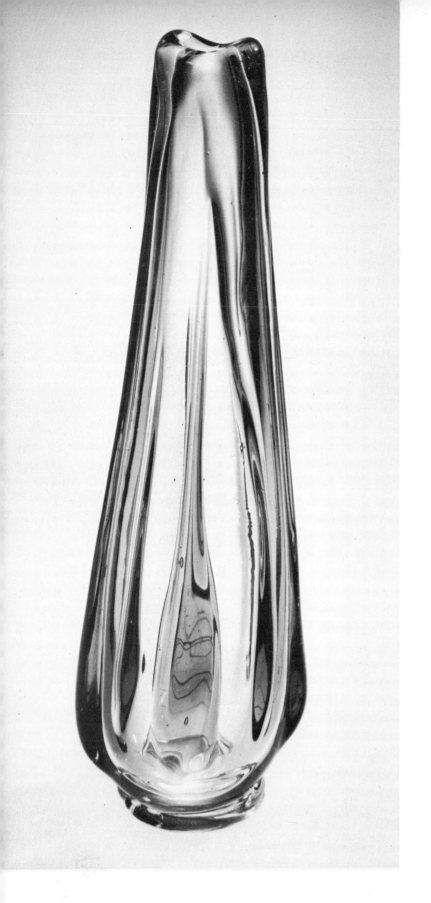

both the University of Wisconsin Research Committee and the Toledo Museum of Art in the project.

The University of Wisconsin granted me salary support for the summer of 1962, and the Toledo Museum, through its director, Otto Whittmann, sponsored two seminars on the museum grounds to bring together those interested, using the technical resources of Toledo as a glass center and the museum's glass collection as an historical reference point. With my furnace and tools, and with suggestions and material from Dominick Labino, then Vice President and Director of Research of Johns Manville's Glass Fibers Division, we melted our first really successful glass and worked it out individually.

Another milestone in my development as a glass artist was my meeting Erwin Eisch in August 1962. My wife and I were in Europe visiting the schools that were reputed to be teaching glassworking with the hot glass available to the students. We attempted to visit the Glasfachschule in Zweisel, West Germany, five miles from the Czech border, but it was closed for vacation. Seeking information at the showroom and cutting house of Kristal-Rimpler, we noticed a piece that was decidedly different from the other work and were told that it had been made at the Eisch factory in nearby Frauenau. In the office were other Eisch pieces, much more expressionistic and very exciting to me.

On visiting the plant we were introduced to Erwin Eisch and to a room full of his fanciful pieces. Meeting Erwin confirmed my belief that glass could be a medium for direct expression by an individual. Although he worked in a factory and with help, he finished all of his pieces himself. Today he has his own furnace—a small, oil-fired, two-pot, fire-breathing monster—in the basement of the factory and a coal-gas-fired periodic brick annealing oven. He can now work every day and has two assistants who turn out his expressionistic goblets and mugs when he is not working on more individual pieces.

THREE PIECES BY THE AUTHOR
FOR THE 1964 MILAN TRIENNALE.

I reported Eisch's activities in *Craft Horizons* in 1963. Erwin came to the First World Crafts Council meeting at Columbia University in June 1964, and with me taught a class in the glass laboratory at the University of Wisconsin. He was my guest at this time—and again in 1967. We lived glass so intensely that my wife threatened divorce on the grounds of abandonment.

Museum recognition came for me in 1963 with a one-man show at The Art Institute of Chicago. Other encouragement came with early, and perhaps premature, exhibitions, including a one-man show in New York in January 1964 at The Museum of Contemporary Crafts and an invitational exhibition in Boston in 1965 at the Society of Arts and Crafts. These led to the establishment in the fall of 1966 of a competitive biennial exhibition, The Toledo Glass National, at the Toledo Museum of Art.

Such museum and university support, and the challenge laid down by Michael and Frances Higgins, Paul Perrot, and others at the Lake George Conference were essential in my early endeavors. It is these institutions and people who are responsible for my involvement with glass, and they who have made this book possible.

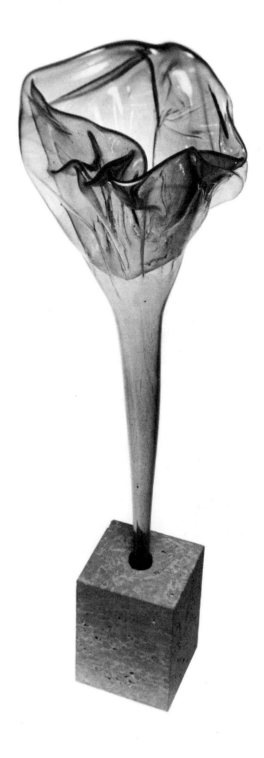

Left:
GLASS FORM BY THE AUTHOR, 1964.

Above:
BLUE FLOWER FORM BY THE AUTHOR, 1965.

1 Form, Glass, & the Artist

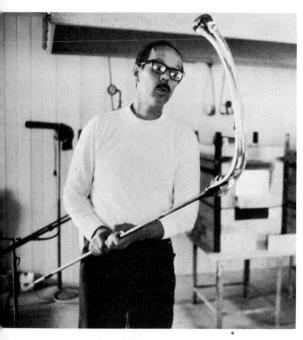

THE AUTHOR WITH A TUBE ON THE BLOWPIPE.

Opposite:
"PARTIALLY RELEASED TENSIONS,"
COPPER-BLUE TUBES
BY THE AUTHOR, 1969.

Essential to the artist's work with glass is his understanding of the material and the basic, elemental, subconscious action-reaction of man and material, not only in the forming of the hot glass—the melting and the forming—but in the complete integration of man and material in a totally controlled time-space concept. The artist must know the glass as it is melting in the furnace—the amalgamation of the inert powders that make up its formulation into the clear glowing stuff he gathers onto his hot iron. He must know it through his hands as they manipulate it with his tools to influence the shape, through the re-heating and periodic chilling of the shape as it is growing and cooling, to the point of finishing it by cutting away the superfluous, or adding it to the assemblage that makes up his form statement.

To keep each phase an individually rewarding source and probe continually its implication are basic to the dynamics of form evolution in any material. It is a necessity of the creative life to seek new personal form-vision with each experience, to make each form based on its own unique and ever-changing standards. The method used by the contemporary artist is a constant probing and questioning of the standards of the past and the definitions of the present to find an opening for new form statements in the material and the process. It is even said that this search is the end in itself.

Although knowledge of chemistry or physics as they apply to glass will broaden the artist's possibilities, it cannot create them. Tools can be made, furnaces and annealing ovens can be built cheaply. But it is through the insatiable, adventurous urge of the artist to discover the essence of glass that his own means of expression will emerge.

The basic purpose of this book is to reveal a few primary facts about offhand glassblowing, and to point out sources to consult as problems arise so that the artist working in glass can think about them and perhaps make use of them in this work. I do not wish to indicate any single direction, but instead to point up the broad spectrum of possibility. The discovery of form is always personal and crucial. Form, the artist's intention expressed through the essence of his material, is always revealed in crisis and prepared in an intimate exploration of the material. This requires the kind of understanding that begins where this book must end.

Aesthetically, one of the values of a finished glass article is found in its modulation of light, white and colored, which illumines and extends its form. An article of glass embodies the moment of its invention. The translation of light into illuminated form in glass ought to be a natural expression of the molten glass and the methods used to shape the piece. The methods, as well as the spirit infusing the method, combine to give the organic sense of the piece and should be as evident in glass as they are in painting. The history of the article, which is the artist's experience with it, should be inescapably apparent to the knowledgeable viewer.

The artists in glass today have generally come to glass from other arts. They have been sculptors, potters, painters, jewelers, poets, and mathematicians. The good ones encounter glass because they want to know what glass is—what they can do with it, and what it can do for them.

Glass is static only when the piece has been completed, when there is nothing more to be done with it. When the artist lifts his blowpipe, he must be prepared to intervene with all his aptitude, training, form-sense, as well as physical and mental energy. Everything he knows converges at once on this curious scene reenacted millions of times in human history: a man breathing his desire into the molten glass. Each time it recurs it is only as different as the men are different from one another; the dance with the blowpipe, the sudden grasping of tools and the hissing of steam as they are applied, the form completed—these things remain the same. A man cannot educe forms from hot glass by conceiving it as a cold, finished material. He must see it hot on the end of his pipe as it emerges glowing from the furnace; he must have a sense of wonder! His perceptions are ever new; his reactions must be swift and decisive! He must immerse himself in immediate experimentation and study, for the glass will not wait.

In glassblowing, if the necessary risk is taken, the outcome must always be in doubt. Artistic creation must occur in crisis, it cannot be planned or divided up; a blistered, mottled, collapsed, unidentifiable handblown glass object may be more valuable than a crystal swan. This principle is fundamental in the training of the glass artist.

The traditional method of learning to form glass has been through the apprentice system. But this system prolongs the development of the apprentice's artistry by limiting him to one phase in the production of glass. This training could not prepare anyone to function as an independent artist, but only to serve as a cog in the industrial machinery. There is not any one thing that *must* be learned first in blowing glass.

"DISTORTION BOX," BENT PLATE GLASS, BY THE AUTHOR, 1970.

To divide what should be a single unbroken act of artistry into a series of functions is to destroy it. Manufactured glass is, for this reason, an expression of the industrial rather than of the artistic process. The great manufacturing firms invest their resources in tens of thousands of products ranging from casserole dishes and light bulbs to radiation shields, laser glass, and great sheets for building facades. Because their technical and commercial requirements are extremely demanding, the standards which govern the glass permit no impurity, no blemish, no flaw in the finished product.

The pride of the companies in the purity of their glass carries over into the design and manufacture of "art glass"—crystal objects, decorative birds and animals, and sculptures—which are invariably executed in bright and perfectly clear glass to appeal on a mass rather than on an individual basis. The designer begins with what the glass industry calls its "brilliant pure crystal." Then a team of factory craftsmen executes the design. Inevitably, the article that emerges is of less interest in itself than it is as an emblem of the process which produced it. The history of the article is not seen as the artist's individual experience, but as the successful completion of various technological steps, with the designer serving as one step.

The factory art-glass designer is a draftsman, tracing lines on his drawing board which will be methodically transferred by a craftsman and given life by industry. He is frustrated by both the peculiar misplacement of his skill, and his inclusion in a process where little experimentation or interference is permitted.

Art relies very little on the kind of inspiration that precedes the work, or the stylistic concepts laid down as company policy. The result is that more and more artists are entering colleges and universities where they can work independently as artists and teachers with adequate resources and compensation, instead of going into industry as designers. Prototypes for movements of this kind can be found in the British art schools in the period following industrialization. With the failure of the Arts and Crafts movement to integrate the artist into either the industrial process or communities of revolutionary artists, many adherents of this philosophy turned to the art schools. Something similar is occurring in the United States, where government appropriations for the arts, foundation grants, and growing public support for the arts are providing places for artists in expanding university departments and schools of art. These schools are devoted to undergraduate and graduate instruction and the unhampered development of art, and are not to be confused with the professional art schools which prepare artists, craftsmen, and designers for commercial or industrial occupations. The college or university art school offers the artist the opportunity to take a long view, to experiment, develop forms, and work without feeling that he must freeze his conception so it can be packaged and produced.

There are other advantages to the university art department. Workshops, laboratories, equipment, and supplies can be provided far better in the university than in the private art schools or in one's own studio. Higher salaries and the security of the tenure system, though not without their difficulties, provide a much better living and greater freedom of expression than the traditional patronage system. Economically and socially the artist has found a home. The results have already been seen in production on a larger scale, expansion into new media, and greater freedom. There is truly an art explosion. Any good university or college art department is swamped by faculty and student applications.

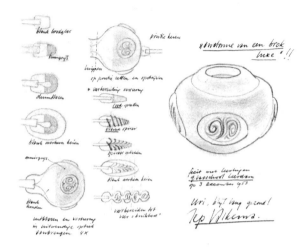

THIS SKETCH BY SYBREN VALKEMA OF THE STEP-BY-STEP CREATION OF A PIECE SEEMS TO BELIE THE IMMEDIACY OF THE ARTISTIC PROCESS IN GLASS. THE FINISHED PIECE IS REMARKABLY LIKE THE SKETCH.

The role of the artist-teacher is an interesting one. The expression he gives his ideas will be valuable to his students, but less important than a clear, forcible awakening in them of the adventurous artistic spirit. The teacher should remember as he progresses in his own work that glass is still essentially unexplored. The material itself has depths of which we have only intimations: methods of display, lighting, the combination of glass with other materials in sculpture are questions which have scarcely been touched upon. So the student must be encouraged to go in his own direction. Everything depends on the student's own discovery of the inherent qualities of glass through his own experimentation. The teacher must at times remain as noncommittal as a Zen master; while at other times he must act decisively to discourage facile or imitative work.

It is impossible to predict which students will continue to work in glass—to succeed as glass artists. The most brilliantly promising sometimes simply disappear or quit without any apparent reason or explanation. Others, who develop more slowly, may work profoundly with glass when they reach maturity. The teacher's primary obligation is to reveal for each student the full, unhindered range of creative possibilities available in glass. Once the student has adopted some discernible direction, the teacher can advise him of the implications and potentials of his course, illustrate techniques which might enhance his growth, and discuss the pertinent technology with him. In this way the student will begin to understand what is happening in his work, where the pitfalls lie, and what his possibilities are.

Students of art come from every corner of the university student body. Some want a little art flavor in their education, or a relief from their intensive studies in science or mathematics. Many are serious, vocation-oriented students who bring an intensive, demanding concentration to their study. Many make great sacrifices to pursue their field, leaving other more materially rewarding pursuits to be in the arts. One must admire these young, and not-so-young, people for their dedication. Any attempt to spoonfeed, to ladle out measured doses of study based on past experience or values, soon meets with intense opposition. Any attempt to hide information, for whatever reason, meets with contempt. Students think nothing of going off independently to wherever they think they might find the information, be it on a weekend trip or a year in Europe. They search out industrial techniques and materials as easily as they turn in a history term paper. Being involved with them is rewarding and exhausting— though at times I can believe that the measured lessons of the old system would be a great relief.

The point is that because of these students we can look forward to continuing exploitation of and exploration in glass. As an example, one student with a background in engineering, who worked as a designer for a manufacturer of air conditioners, returned to the university for his Master of Fine Arts in Printmaking. He became interested in glass and after some months in the studio, he brought in some of his deep-etched copperplates, wiped them with a glass enamel, and took an intaglio print with a gather of hot glass. It was a direct reaction and occurred because there was no demand on him except that he pursue *something* to an end.

There has been some eclecticism and some sensationalism to date in glass, but, tempting as it might be to dismiss much of the work on this basis, it must be understood that we are only seeing the first generation of university-trained artists. These creative young people will be continually expanding our horizons in glass, and we look forward with great excitement and security to our future.

EXHIBIT OF WORKS BY ERWIN EISCH
IN STUTTGART, 1962.

Economic opportunity is not automatically ruled out if the glass artist does not go into industry or teaching. There is now, with our built-in inflation, a great desire to invest in art works. The growth of glass collections and the increased number of people willing to collect works of living artists have worked strongly in the artist's favor. The scarcity of Tiffany glass has forced the collectors of this highly treasured glass into new areas. The reception in the art market of even the earliest attempts of the glass artist in America has been almost phenomenal. Long before the work merited sale there was a clamor for it. By 1968 the exhibitions, galleries, and critics were well aware of the movement, giving the recognition so important to the maturation of the field. I would not hesitate to recommend the setting up of independent studios and I would expect early acceptance of mature and individual work in the art market. One must realize that as the museum directors, gallery directors, and critics grow more sophisticated in their judgments of the new glass, collectors will become more discriminating in their purchases. But in measure they will be willing to make greater commitments in the amount of money spent for their purchases. I would sincerely hope that as this commitment grows, the artist will develop a creative, individual concept and will place emphasis on the individual piece rather than on the number of units produced.

It would be ideal if the collectors would recognize the importance of their purchases in the development of the field and would educate themselves in the drives and attitudes of the glass artist so that they can demand the best, thus making it possible for the artist to give them the best. In this way their purchases will be more valuable, and the artist will grow in the measure of the opportunity offered. The artist invites the participation of the knowledgeable public in the growth of the field and treasures the personal relationships established between himself and his collectors.

2 Backgrounds

Why speak of history at all? Like everyone else in these strange, disconnected times, we inherit a great deal which is irrelevant. We have a comprehension of a world which is threatened at every turn. We are resolute in the intelligibility of our work today and in little else. Why dust off William Morris, John Ruskin, Emile Gallé, and Louis Comfort Tiffany?

One measure of an artist's insecurity is his desire to find in his own work the culmination of those who preceded him. One may also question, however, whether the originality of the artist has been exhausted when he must rely so heavily on tradition or in claiming progenitors. What aspects of history should be considered important to the artist interested in or already working with glass?

The modern glass artist, like any artist, is always free to revoke or recast his tradition, choosing from among his predecessors in the milieux of Rome, Bohemia, Murano, or those who regenerated a vital new art form from the chaos of the industrial revolution. But because the most valuable techniques and processes employed before industrialization have been discovered anew and refined in the last ninety years, he probably will profit more by concentrating his historical attention on the great artists of the modern tradition. These men sought new kinds of beauty and new methods of achieving it. They differed from their predecessors and are more pertinent to our own period because they were trained artists who became involved with glass out of fascination with its possibilities rather than as an extension of family involvement, or out of local tradition. While this is generally true for all contemporary artist-craftsmen, it is doubly true for the artist who works in molten glass, an art so completely eclipsed by machinery and the machine mentality.

The movement in the arts which began with John Ruskin and William Morris could not have ignored the forces that had caused the devaluation of the traditional handicrafts. In theory it was unruly and insurgent in its revolt against industrialism and the diminution of the quality of life in the industrial West. Integrated, individual art was set against the machine process. By demonstrating vitality, passion, intellect, taste, and skill, the artist-craftsman who joined this movement tried to impose order on the growing shambles.

John Ruskin, whose influence on the conscience of Victorian England was extremely strong, believed that the decline of art and taste in a society was a sign of a general cultural crisis, and that to awaken man's sense of beauty the conditions under which he lived must be changed.

William Morris—poet, painter, decorator, and former member of the Little Birmingham Group at Oxford which was devoted to Ruskin—used the master's doctrines in his analysis of the industrial techniques which had undercut the preindustrial aesthetic. Until the French Revolution, the high standards of the guilds made it virtually impossible for anyone to obtain poorly made implements of any kind. The dissolution of the guilds left the newly risen factory owners to decide how glassware—as well as everything else—should be designed and manufactured. The result was an unstoppable flood of cheaply made, badly decorated merchandise. The Arts and Crafts Movement attempted to counteract this flood through its creative work in furniture, wallpaper, hangings, carpet weaving, tile painting, carving, stained glass, textiles, and metalwork. While Morris and his colleagues succeeded in stimulating original craftsmanship in Britain, most adherents of the movement eventually gave up the idea of fighting the industrial world and accepted the iron domination of the machine.

Opposite:
SUPERB VASE BY EMILE GALLÉ, c. 1900,
SHOWING HIS INTEREST IN INSECTS AND PLANTS.
(COURTESY OF THE CORNING MUSEUM OF GLASS.)

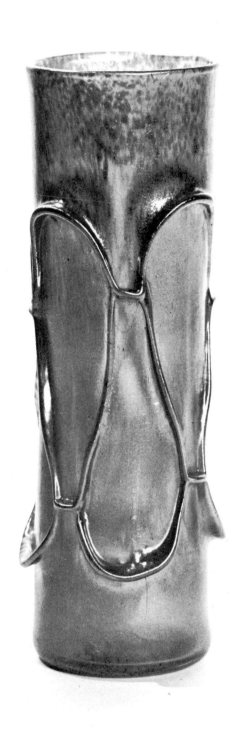

Nevertheless, between 1884 and 1894, while the founders of "L'art Moderne" were showing their first works in the galleries in Brussels, William Morris's successors in Great Britain—men like Arthur H. Macmurdo and C. R. Ashbee—were discarding Morris's dislike for modern machines and business methods. They began promoting the so-called minor arts through organizations like the Art Workers Guild (1884) and the Arts and Crafts Exhibition Society (1888). Their belief that the decorative arts could be as profoundly moving as painting would find root elsewhere.

Coursing within the broader tradition of the Arts and Crafts Movement, woven into it though not explicitly concerned with social issues, were the traditions of the continental glassmakers—Gallé, Lalique, Marinot—and of Tiffany and Carder in the United States. Revivalists, originators, innovators, and at the same time eclectic, these artists uncovered and developed processes of glassmaking and decoration unused for decades. In their work, scientific knowledge and technical skills were subordinated to artistic form-sense developed to varying degrees of perfection. The unsurpassed delicacy of form and color of Tiffany's *Favrile* shows how successful this convergence can be. Their work supplied the glass revival with its real vitality.

Much of their important work in glass has been lumped together and inaccurately labeled as "Art Nouveau." Rather than being an offshoot, these works were conceived before the style was named and were still being created after its demise and with the rise of Cubism, Post-Impressionism, Fauvism, Futurism, and the various other movements of the first two decades of the twentieth century. Art Nouveau as an integration of all arts and architecture is currently being restudied and reevaluated. The classification of all glass from 1880 - 1920 as Art Nouveau is not very accurate. It had its own vitality and its own motivations.

Emile Gallé was a decorator, cabinetmaker, potter, poet, botanist, and orator as well as an artist in glass. His fantastically colored glass would deeply impress Louis Comfort Tiffany when he viewed it in 1889. After attending the art school at Weimar, Gallé completed his education in Paris and in London, where he studied applied arts at the Victoria and Albert Museum and botany at Kew Gardens. In 1874 he returned to Nancy, where his father had a faïence factory. There he began producing his first examples of enameled glass. He increased his botanical and biological knowledge by making detailed studies of flowers, animals, and insects which he incorporated into his glass forms. For decoration Gallé preferred "sturdy homely plants like the thistle and the oak." As he progressed, his botanical observations were combined with his study of Japanese art to achieve evermore delicately fantastic effects.

Gallé gave cameo glass freedom of design, linear form, and botanical accuracy. He broke away from classical stylization of plant forms and combined the botanical accuracy with Japanese spatial feeling. The asymmetrical and sinuous movement of his plant forms encompasses the vase form and embraces it.

To get the full impact of the breadth of his work, one must visit the museum of the École de Nancy in Nancy, France. There the full flood of his creative force is assembled in room after room of the house of a wealthy merchant who donated it to the city as a museum. We have all seen a few examples of the cameo style, acid cut-back, vases that made up the bulk of his later production. But it is far more im-

Left:
CYLINDRICAL VASE BY GALLÉ.
THE ENAMELING AND THE STYLIZED FLOWERS
ARE TYPICAL OF HIS EARLY WORK.
(COLLECTION OF THE AUTHOR.)

Center:
GALLÉ VASE IN CAMEO TECHNIQUE.
(COURTESY OF THE ART INSTITUTE
OF CHICAGO.)

Right:
CAMEO VASE BY GALLÉ.
(COLLECTION OF SIMEON HENNINGER.)

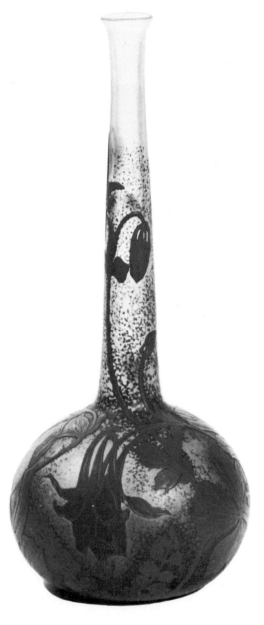

portant to see his full range of expression in an integrated surrounding, including some of his furniture, than to study a few isolated examples of the stereotyped work that is to be found in most collections. His range was tremendous; his vision helped to shape a style and transcend it.

Gallé, like Tiffany, Carder, Lalique, and others of their period, was financially able to undertake the construction of a small glass factory for the production of his own work. But as the industry and capital continued to grow and combine, the factories tended to become larger and larger, beyond the scope of individual control. Since the glass industry was one of the first to mechanize, Gallé could not help but be affected by the creeping giantism of the industry. In 1900, a museum director mourned the loss of the more ''genuine and personal'' style of Gallé's earlier collections.

Three years before his death in 1904, Gallé started a school at Nancy offering instruction in glass-making and other arts and crafts, but his intricate, lyrical conception could not be imparted directly to his students. After his death the quality of articles his craftsmen produced declined so rapidly that the glassworks was closed within a few years. But the Daum brothers, Alsatians who became admirers of Gallé when they moved their family glassworks to Nancy, continued to produce excellent original glass, retaining their individual style while absorbing Gallé's influence.

René Lalique, a distinguished Parisian jeweler, devoted himself wholly to ''the enchanted substance which is glass'' after the turn of the century. Lalique was born at Aix-en-Champagne and educated at the École des Arts Décoratifs. He opened a jewelry shop on the Place Vendôme, where he made amazing glass jewels like uncut cabochons. This began his discovery of glass. With the assistance of four glassmakers he produced a series of scent bottles to help him ''learn the trade.'' Satisfied that he could master it, Lalique bought a glassworks in 1918 at Wingen-sur-Moder near the German border, equipped it with modern apparatus, and devoted himself to technical research and production. Until his assistants were trained, he modeled his own molds and did his own cutting and engraving. Afterward he confined his efforts to designing and modeling. Lalique's door panels were embellished with scrolls, spirals, and truncated pyramids. He explored many possibilities in sculpture, reliefs, and lost-wax methods. The pieces made at the height of his production have a delightful slight opalescence in the heavy parts of the modeling. This was lost in later ''pure crystal'' pieces.

Above:
OPALESCENT VASE BY RENÉ LALIQUE, MOLD-BLOWN.
(COURTESY OF THE ART INSTITUTE OF CHICAGO.)

Right:
GREEN MOLD-BLOWN VASE BY LALIQUE,
WITH ACID-ETCHED DEPRESSIONS AND
POLISHED RIM. (COURTESY OF THE ART INSTITUTE
OF CHICAGO.)

Maurice Marinot was a recognized painter and one of the original members of the Fauves, the "Savages." In 1911 he went to visit his friends the Viard brothers, who owned a glassworks at Bar-sur-Seine, not far from Marinot's home in Troyes. There he saw possibilities in glassblowing for artistic form-statement as diverse as those in sculpture and painting. His fascination with glass began at the age of thirty, a time when most artists would hesitate to attempt mastery of a new field. But his enthusiasm was so great that the Viard brothers gave him a corner of the factory to work out his designs and access to all the facilities during the lunch hour.

Marinot, more than any artist before him, foretold the directions of our own time. When he became dissatisfied with the factory-produced forms, he taught himself, with the aid of the skilled workers, to blow his own glass. By 1920 he was able to control his pieces, giving them the full range of expression under the guidance and inspiration of his own hands and breath.

Though also influenced by nature, Marinot did not reproduce or imitate its forms as surface decoration in the style of Gallé. His inspiration found expression in sculpturesque forms, these "naked and muscular pieces," some with enamel marvered between layers of transparent glass, others deeply etched in acid or shaped with grinding wheels. Though he did make perfume bottles and vase shapes, he was opposed to the concept of "industrial design" coming into fashion at this time, saying that any thought of his glass serving a useful purpose was abhorrent to him.

Recognition of his work came as early as 1913, when the French government bought a small goblet which he had designed for the Musée de Luxembourg.

Above:
MARINOT VASE WITH FURNACE-WORKED DECORATION,
DONE WHILE THE GLASS WAS SOFT. (COURTESY OF
THE VICTORIA AND ALBERT MUSEUM.)

Right:
DEEP PURPLE VASE BY JEAN SALA,
A TYPICAL HANDLING OF THE MATERIAL.
(COURTESY OF THE ART INSTITUTE OF CHICAGO.)

In 1937 the Viard factory closed down, and Marinot went back to his painting—never to return to glass. His total production of glass pieces amounted to 2,500 pieces—not a great number by glass standards. It is not their scarcity which led to his work's value, rather it is Marinot's concept of glass, as seen in his work, and as expressed in this excerpt from his unpublished autobiography:

...to preserve, within a given form, the robust nobility of the hot, thick glass ready to be blown, and while blowing it, to let the nature of the glass assert itself, to control its natural tendencies without denying them: while the glass is at the height of its incandescence, to coax from it forms that are plump and yielding, and then to incorporate into them other pieces evoking still or running water, or crackling and melting ice.

Though he lived until 1960, Marinot's reputation as a painter was never reestablished. Most of his paintings and drawings were destroyed during World War II. His reputation is inextricably linked to glass in which he cut and etched his forms, and added many colored inclusions between gathers.

The "brightness and transparency" of Marinot's glass, melted in the factory, contrasts sharply with the glass of Jean Sala.

Jean Sala produced glass which is coarse and impure. These characteristics were due in large part to insufficient melting and firing. But Sala, following the traditions of the ancient craft learned from his Catalonian father, worked alone in a small atelier in the Montparnasse district of Paris. He stopped production in 1947 when his eyes could no longer stand the brilliance of the furnace. His tools and techniques were the ancient, traditional ones used by all glassblowers throughout time. Sala's forms were simple and direct, well adapted to his glass quality, with applied glass decoration of swans, grapes, and other natural forms.

Although he was part of the artistic community in Montparnasse, Sala is now using his studio to re-build Spanish antiquities, which are sold in his shop on the Rue Bonaparte near the École des Beaux Arts. His son began to work with him in glass, but found none of the interest that had moved his father, and is now managing the antique shop. At this writing Jean Sala is an active man of around seventy years who travels to his native Spain each year to purchase pieces for his shop.

In America, Louis Comfort Tiffany of the great merchandising family of New York City is now the subject of a major revival. Tiffany came to glass from an art background and exerted powerful individual control on his glassworks. His work is the most striking example of what we have lost in today's design of industrially produced "art" glass. His dramatic sense of form was translated directly into the material, whether glass or bronze. Looking back on his career, observing the survival of his reputation, one is struck by the fact that the studied connoisseurship of the museum and dealers is not primarily responsible for his continuing popularity. It is the dedicated and enthusiastic amateur collector, educated and aware, who collected Tiffany glass and modern art. The great collection of Joseph Heil, recently donated to the Museum of Modern Art, is indicative of this trend.

Although the Art Nouveau feeling found expression in much of Tiffany's delicately sinuous glass, his work spanned the Art Nouveau period, both anticipating and outliving its curvilinear ornament and

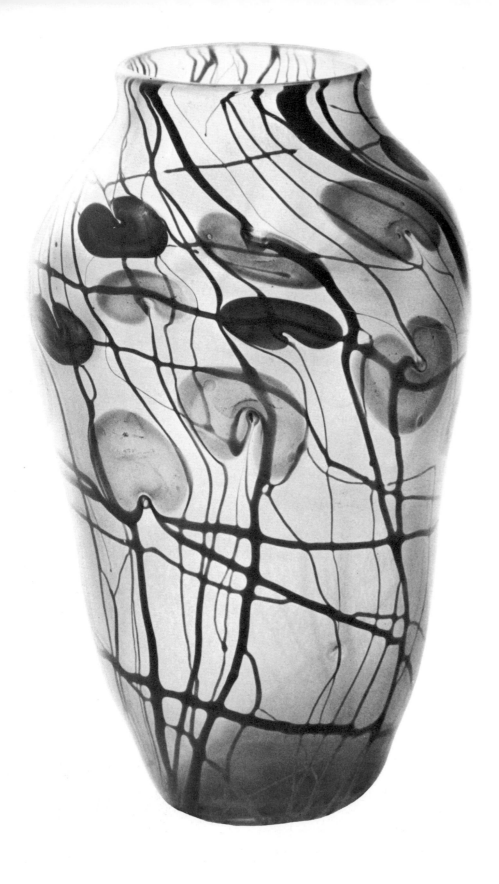

TIFFANY VASE.
(COLLECTION OF SIMEON HENNINGER.)

Opposite—
Top left:
TIFFANY FLOWER-FORM VASE AND GOBLET, *c.* 1900.
(COLLECTION OF JOSEPH HEIL.)

Top center:
A PARTICULARLY FINE VASE BY MAURICE MARINOT, *c.* 1920.
(COURTESY OF THE ART INSTITUTE OF CHICAGO.)

Top right:
TWO JACK-IN-THE-PULPIT VASES BY TIFFANY.

Bottom left:
BOWL BY JEAN SALA, *c.* 1910.
(COURTESY OF THE ART INSTITUTE OF CHICAGO.)

Bottom right:
BOWL THAT REFLECTS GREEN AND TRANSMITS RED,
BY FRANCOIS DECORCHEMENT, AFTER 1920.
(COURTESY OF THE ART INSTITUTE OF CHICAGO.)

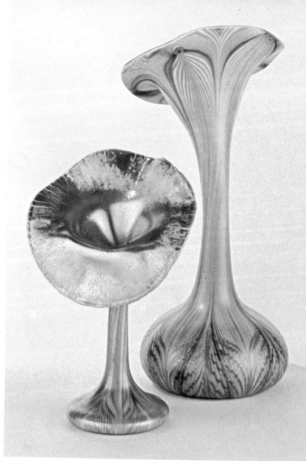

plant-derived outlines. Tiffany's freedom of ornamentation on the surface of his glass and the integration of form, color, and design was unsurpassed in the world of glass in his time. He exercised very tight control over the output of his studios, and though there were some dull mold-blown shapes, the vast majority bore his personal stamp. Tiffany attenuated many of his forms, giving a sense of very personal proportion. Certainly, his bronze forms were beautifully conceived for the metal and must have influenced his reaction to glass. His oversize "flower form" goblets have an almost metallic look.

A much more extensive discussion of Tiffany and his influence would be warranted by his status in American glass. However, comprehensive studies are already available. There is a book forthcoming on Frederick Carder, but little has been done biographically on Marinot, Lalique, Gallé, or Sala.

Frederick Carder, an English glass designer for Stevens and Williams, was trained as a sculptor. An ambiguous figure in the history of modern glass, he migrated to the United States in 1903 and founded the Steuben Glassworks. Although he personally preferred neoclassical work, he duplicated the techniques made famous by others: Tiffany's iridescent and peacock designs, Marinot's heavy bottles, Laliques's cast crystal with acid etching, Roman millefiore bowls, the cameo vases of nineteenth-century Britain and Gallé. He possessed a "classic" but highly individualized sense of proportion with a Sung quietness of volume relationships—a combination which barely avoided the frozen, dead, mechanical forms of his time, but was still beautiful. It is valuable to study Carder, who began as a designer in England at the height of Gallé's influence, witnessed the rise of Tiffany, and began his own factory—working at the same time as Lalique and Marinot and sustaining his capabilities in production over some eighty years. He died at the age of one hundred in 1963. He is the subject of a comprehensive new study by Paul Gardner, Curator of Glass and Ceramics at the Smithsonian Institution, who served as his assistant for more than thirteen years.

Left:
VASE BY LOETZ, *c.* 1900.
THE PEACOCK MOTIF WITH FEATHER THREADING
WAS POPULARIZED BY TIFFANY. (COLLECTION
OF SIMEON HENNINGER.)

BLUE AURENE COMPOTE (ABOVE) AND
VERRE DE SOIE CANDLESTICKS (BELOW)
BY FREDERICK CARDER. (COLLECTION OF THE AUTHOR.)

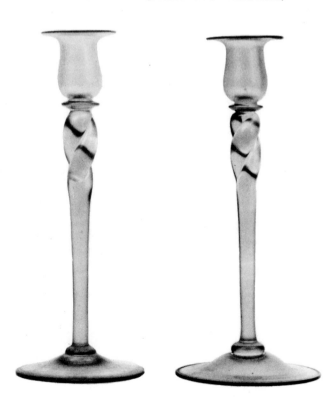

In the United States there is a wide gap between the early 1900s—with Tiffany's *Favrile* glass and similar "art glass"—and the seminar-workshop sponsored by the Toledo Museum of Art in 1962 where the revival of offhand glassblowing started a national movement. With the exception of Frederick Carder, individual work in the studio was a lost art. Those artists who worked independently in glass during this time served to preserve but not always to advance traditional methods. Maurice Heaton enameled and bent flat glass; Marianne V. Allesch designed tableware and decorative panels with painted abstractions; Frances and Michael Higgins produced their laminated, interdecorated, sagged forms; others produced during this time; but the most significant fact is that none of these artists penetrated to the heart of glasswork—they did not work with molten glass directly from the furnace. They seemed to find themselves stranded between an industrial technology and a true artistic exploration of this fascinating material. This might be explained by the overshadowing dominance of the great manufacturers of glass.

The movement beginning with the Society of Arts and Crafts in England led to the formation of schools dedicated to the revival of the skills and values supposedly inherent in medieval craftsmanship, with the goal of somehow influencing the manufacturers of machine-produced goods to accept these values. In Germany, one of the foremost leaders of the Art Nouveau movement, the Belgian architect Henry Van De Velde, was invited to take over the Arts and Crafts Institute and the Academy of Fine Art at Weimar in 1902. In 1919, on his recommendation, Walter Gropius, a leading young architect, was invited to take over the leadership of the school.

The term "Bauhaus" was used originally to define the community of workers who made the great edifices of the Middle Ages, and was symbolic to Gropius of the techniques and the artistry brought together in these architectural masterpieces. To develop the builders of tomorrow he proposed a system to bring together the industrial technicians and the artists who, together, would encompass the complexities of modern building technology and decoration until the new breed was available. This educational principle of teaching an art or craft with two disconnected and detached "masters," as was the case in the early Bauhaus, has never been fully assessed. Since teachers who understood both art and the new industrial technology were not available, Paul Klee, for instance, was invited to give criticism in weaving. Gerhard Marks, the sculptor, gave criticism in ceramics along with a "technical master" from industry. The polarity of the teachers' viewpoints allowed the student the greatest leeway. He was able to accept or reject what he wished from each master and to assume his own position in his field with whatever emphasis he wished. He was free to demand assistance, but there was no strong direction exemplified or demanded.

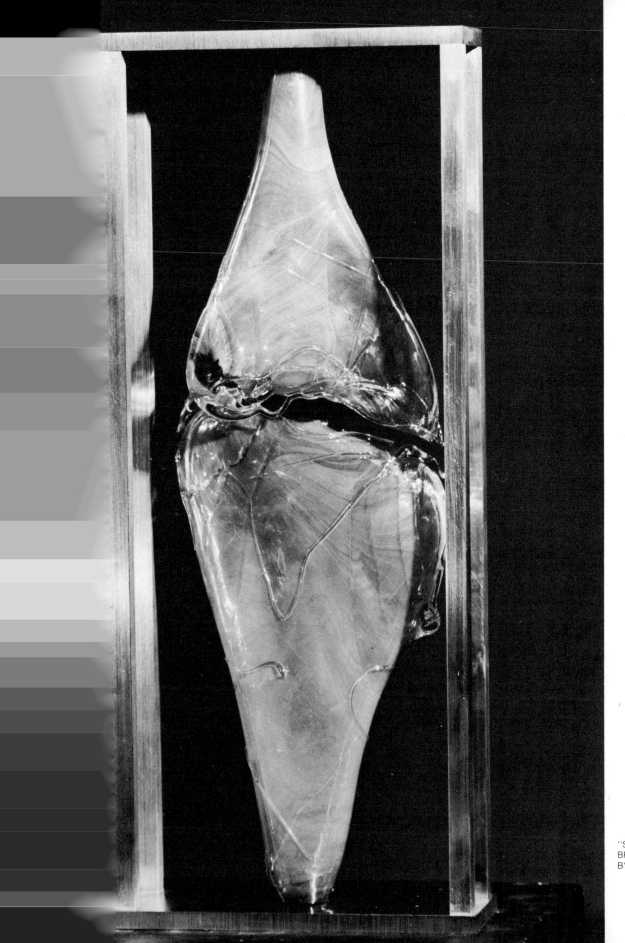

"SYMPHONY IN YELLOW,"
BRASS AND STEEL FRAME WITH BLOWN SILVER GLASS,
BY THE AUTHOR, 1966. (COLLECTION OF THE AUTHOR.)

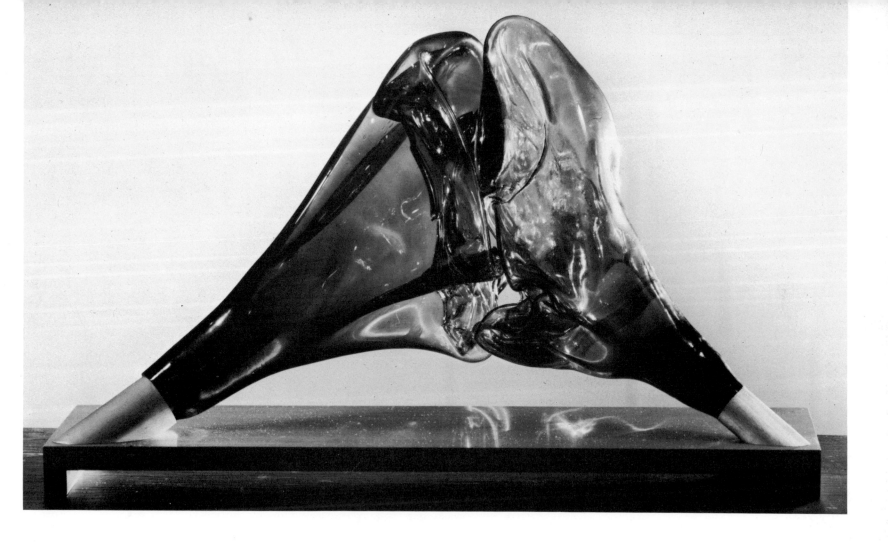

"RED FORMS IN OPPOSITION,"
COPPER RED GLASS WITH BRASS FITTINGS
AND BASE, BY THE AUTHOR, 1966.

The result produced strong individual personalities, but not the integrated community of Gropius's original vision. Instead, the design problems in the initial trial period of the Bauhaus, which were used to test the creative aptitude of the potential students, have been enshrined in a great number of art schools as a frozen series of principles, as incontrovertible dogma. I cannot estimate the effect of the Bauhaus education on modern architecture, but I can say that its teachings have been perverted in the creation of the term "industrial design."

I have no argument with pleasing form in functional objects. I have no displeasure in using such functionally engineered objects—engineered for production, packaging, and distribution. I enjoy pleasant useful objects, but I cannot conceive that any of these worthy aims is in itself art. The creation of such objects may be a fine profession, but training for such a profession is not the same as, or even comparable to, the education of an artist. The ultimate criteria in industrial design must be the consideration of consumer taste and the adaptability of design form to mass production. These could hardly be equated as criteria when evaluating a work of art as an art object. Consequently, though there may be a superimposition of artistic principles to enhance the world of technology and industry, there cannot be a similar advancement of art through reliance on the principles of technology and industry.

If the artist wishes to ignore social and functional values in evolving his form-statement, it is his right. Any attempt to justify the value of a form because it is functional is often an excuse for a limited or weak form-vision. There is no attempt here to discredit art education or industrial design, but rather to stay with the basics—art unencumbered with social values.

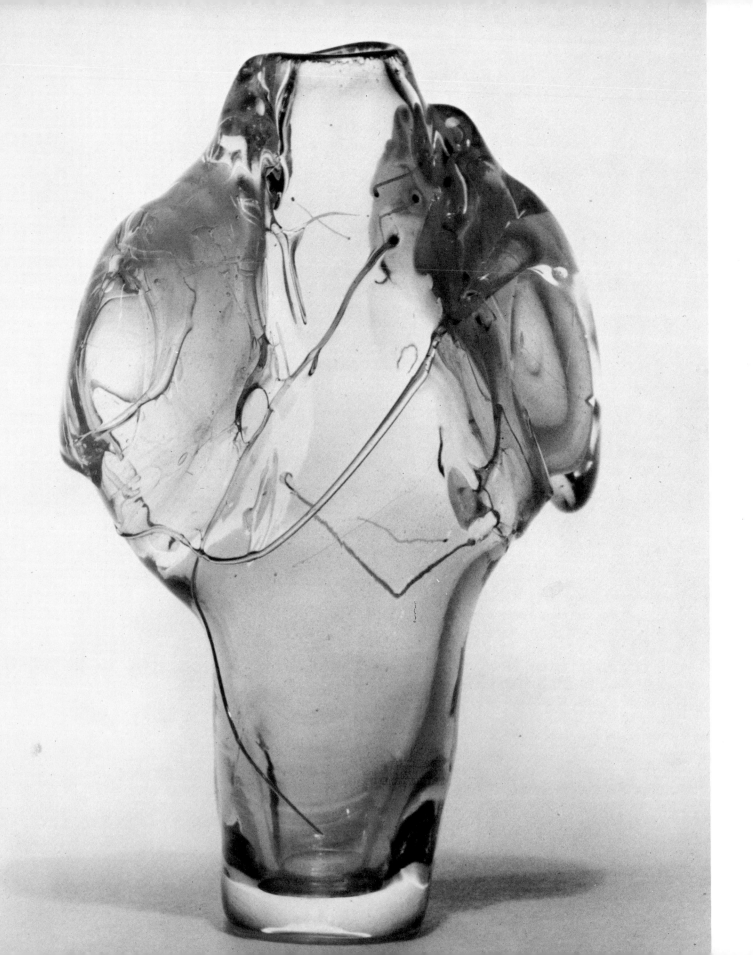

Today we can see that there are three major ways in which professional art departments have developed within higher liberal education in the universities and colleges. The thrust and potential of a department generally is strongly related to the directions from which it came. First the classical humanistic studies, involving the teaching of art history with studio art courses for practical experience, has led to the formation of art departments for the education of practicing artists. Second is, with an understandable concomitant overemphasis, the development of professional schools, such as architecture, with background offerings in studio art. This concept evolved under the influence of the Bauhaus experiment and has contributed to the development of the university "community of artists."

The third major movement has been related to the philosophy that teaching of purely intellectual subjects in general education was one-sided and that visual-tactile senses were important in the education of the "whole man." For the first time the art of children was discovered and admired for its value in helping the child to think out and consciously express his inner life and his experience of the visible environment. This desire to teach self-expression drew an increasing number of artists into the field of primary and secondary education. With the increasing professionalism of education, art education became fixed in the curriculum as a separate discipline. The establishment of schools of education in colleges and universities brought with them departments devoted to art education. With present-day emphasis on content, these departments have sought more and more professional artists to enrich their studio courses, in turn creating numbers of professionally oriented students.

Opposite:
YELLOW ANTHROPOMORPHIC VASE
BY THE AUTHOR, 1965.
(COLLECTION OF MRS. MARK HOOPER.)

Above left:
COPPER SCHMELTZ GLASS FORM
BY THE AUTHOR, 1966.
(COURTESY OF THE SMITHSONIAN INSTITUTION.)

Above right:
SCULPTURE OF BLOWN GLASS,
CUT AND MOUNTED ON A MIRRORED BASE,
BY THE AUTHOR, 1968.
(COLLECTION OF JAMES DILLON.)

Right and Opposite:
TWO WORKS IN CRYSTAL, WITH DECORATION
IN SILVER AND DIAMOND-POINT
BY JOEL PHILIP MYERS.

Art is a factor in the education of the "whole" man. The crafts and arts now mingle freely in the school, college, and university curriculum. The broad social concern of Morris's followers has filtered through, but the emphasis is now on the significance of the artist's search for a truly modern harmony of men and materials. The insistence on the value of individual creativity, the conviction that the artist-craftsman must freely explore his material and himself without restraints or imposed pressures, must remain the indispensible precondition to the development of the artist in general—and the glass artist in particular.

3 The Nature of Glass

In the past, glassmakers were restricted by their locale—one area being known for a particular kind of glass. Venetian glass was and to some extent still is a standard, easily worked high-soda formula with some variations for color. English decorative glass was a high-lead, cut-glass "crystal."

In our time the individual working alone can choose what he needs from all traditions, discarding what he does not want, imitating, and finally surpassing the work of the past. In technology he can be eclectic, and this eclecticism may add to his originality.

The modern artist wishes to control his material—not necessarily ignoring present-day achievements in the process. The enumeration of the physical and chemical properties of glass serves him as it does industry, but the goals are different. The broad range of investigation and experimentation undertaken in the great glass factories does have some value for the artist. His approach, however, allows him to dispense with the industrial emphasis on purity and standardization. The glass artist needs to have an intimate feeling for the possibilities for the growth of form while he is working; he needs to be able to understand what he has done retrospectively, when the object has cooled, the artist has cooled, and the form can be studied. His understanding of glass is both intuitive and cognitive. Who can say how much factual information the artist is employing as he works? How much does sense-memory determine his grasp of form as he examines an object from the annealing oven?

Our approach to physics and chemistry is never solely intellectual. If the artist does not know what he is going to do until he does it, then he never can anticipate his technical requirements. He can satisfy them only when the need arises. His work determines everything. He is exploring not only a material, but himself as well! All that results from a batch is what he does with it. All the possibilities are not exhausted, but his ideas may be.

Many excellent books have been written recently about glass. There is the broad category of the history of glass, with the catalogs of pieces surviving and the fascinating stories of the development of the factories and the men involved. There is also a large body of technical literature dating mainly from the first systematic explorations of glass compositions at Jena in the second half of the nineteenth century.

When reading most of the literature about glass, the artist must remember that it is written primarily for people already in the field, so that many of the basics are taken for granted. It is written for people who are not expected to melt the glass, or, if they do melt it, to work it out. One of the best simple technical books is *Modern Glass Practice* by Samuel R. Scholes, who shepherded a couple of generations of aspiring glass technologists through the program at the New York State College of Ceramics at Alfred, New York. This is the basic technical reference for the glass artist's shelf. The Ceramic Materials Issue of *Ceramic Industry* published each January contains a complete listing of all the materials used in the ceramic industry and their uses in glass. Another technical reference with less application to the artist than the technologist, although it contains excellent descriptions of experimental equipment, is *Glass Research Methods* by Ralph K. Day. This small book, though concentrating on testing methods of glass technologists, might signal some new directions for the artist to pursue. Most of the laboratory melting and test equipment would not be beyond the comprehension of someone with some engineering background.

"It can readily be seen that the chemical composition of glass is not the thing that makes glass 'glass,' since hundreds of thousands of different chemical compositions can be made into glasses," says Robert H. Brill in his article, "A Note on the Scientist's Definition of Glass," in volume IV of the *Journal of Glass Studies.* Basically, glass is described as another state of matter—the "glassy state." Brill says that "the word 'glass' is a generic term, and we should most properly speak of 'glasses' rather than 'glass'; just as we speak of 'metals,' 'textiles,' and 'ceramics.'"

Glass is often described as a supercooled liquid solution of inorganic materials with an amorphous structure. It is brittle, smooth, and hard, but also viscous, flowing, endlessly ductile and responsive. It is brilliant or dull, opaque or transparent, intensely colored or colorless! The words used to describe glass are so contradictory that anyone must wonder that any sense can be made of them. Yet, it is these very contradictions that mean so much to the artist. It is the change from the flowing viscous liquid that sticks and burns to the hard cold glass that breaks and cuts which is endlessly fascinating to the artist. It is also the key to perceiving his own direction. Because glass really has no shape, form, or definite substance, the artist is free to impose upon it his own sense of structure or form statement.

Glass slowly thickens all the way through and hardens over a wide range of temperatures. It does not freeze like water, which solidifies into ice-crystal layers from the outside while the center is still liquid, but it becomes supercooled—there are no crystals. The composition is originally composed of crystalline materials ground finely and melted together—vitrified—but there is no return to the crystal on cooling. If crystals do re-form, we say the glass has devitrified. Devitrification can occur at elevated temperatures. The second glass I ever melted began to form "stones" or balls of crystals the second day in the furnace. The rest of the glass was workable, but there were fine white grains all through it: the glass was beginning to devitrify.

The compositions which may be used for glassware are limited strictly by the tendency of all glass to devitrify. Below a certain temperature range, determined by composition, all commercial silicate glasses are unstable. The upper limit of the range is the "liquidus" temperature, the temperature at which the first crystals will separate on cooling the glass, or at which the last crystals will dissolve when the devitrified glass is heated, always provided that an equilibrium is reached during the operation. Above this temperature the glass cannot devitrify, but if it is held too long in the temperature range immediately below the liquidus, devitrification will eventually take place. The molecules of a molten substance always want to lock themselves together in definite and characteristic patterns on cooling, to assume their crystalline structure. In the case of a good glass with a low liquidus, the molten mixture on cooling becomes so thick as to impede the molecules from forming into patterns and becomes hard in a short enough time that an internal structure cannot form. The liquidus temperature is uniquely fixed by the batch composition. Consequently, a glass with a low liquidus temperature is desirable. Glass marbles of 475 composition by Johns-Manville have a very low liquidus temperature; I have held 475 at barely red heat for more than a week without any "stones" or "scum" appearing, without any devitrification.

Brill states that "glasses, instead of having sharp melting points, soften gradually as the temperature is raised...until at high temperatures they finally become quite fluid. It is this gradual softening over a

TIFFANY VASE, OWNED BY THE AUTHOR.
THIS VASE HAS DEVITRIFIED ON THE INSIDE;
IT BECAME UNSTABLE AT ROOM TEMPERATURE
OVER A PERIOD OF YEARS.

range of several hundred degrees centigrade which makes it convenient to describe glass in terms of viscosities.''

It is the wide viscous range, in which the glass cools from a consistency like honey to a thick, taffy-like material, that makes it possible to work with glass. This broad range of viscosities is called the working range. During this period, the glass, because it is an insulating material, cools slowly, retaining a red heat inside that causes a beautiful glow that is never seen after the piece is finished.

The uneven cooling of glass gives rise to strain between the inner and outer surfaces, which is locked in as the glass reaches the point where the outer surface will no longer move and the inner material is still contracting. The strain is removed by controlled cooling, or annealing. This is one of those technical problems which the artist must understand if he works alone. The terms used by the scientist—''strain point,'' ''annealing point,'' ''softening point,'' and ''working point''—are all related to his description of a specific glass and help him to understand and predict the usefulness of that composition. To the artist, these terms have meaning only empirically: can we control this glass to get a finished piece; can we work the glass and cool it successfully? We do have a built-in ''fudge factor'' because, although there are these specific points for any one glass by definition, in practice there is quite a bit of leeway, and we can compensate for slightly lower annealing temperatures, for example, by giving the piece a longer time in the annealing oven.

All these factors vary with differing glasses because of their differing chemical ingredients in differing proportions. Glasses differ enough so that we do not have to be too exact. In fact, if the glass were perfectly annealed—free of all strain—it would break too easily. A moderate amount of strain, reasonably distributed, gives the necessary strength to allow glass to stand normal use. Eyeglasses, water tumblers, automobile windows, modern glass doors are chilled so as to give them extra strength.

A physical factor acting on the molten glass at all times is the flow of the glass in reaction to the gravitational force. This tendency is usually countered by the rotation of the pipe, which, if done fast enough, sets up its own centrifugal force. Then there is the increase of surface tension with increasing viscosity from lower heat that makes it at all possible to work with the glass on a pipe. The slow cooling of the thicker wall because of the temperature differential between the outside of the wall and its center influences the way form changes occur in response to external pressure. It is this same resistance that allows us to blow at all, the cool skin preventing us from blowing right through the surface.

When casting in a cold mold, it is the increased viscosity on contact which keeps the glass surface from conforming to the sharp changes in the mold surface; but, when the glass is cast in a hot investment mold, it will reproduce the surface exactly. A hot mold must be hot enough so that glass ''wets'' it just as it does the iron on the blowpipe. Generally, when you ladle hot glass into a steel, wooden, or graphite mold, the mold is cold so that the glass will release. Pressing gives better reproduction than simple casting in cold molds, and is the normal production method. In the lost-wax process of casting, using an investment where the mold is filled after burn-out, with cold glass and heated together with the mold, the glass gives a faithful reproduction of the surface.

The ''ductility'' of molten glass is really a function of the working range and the liquidus temperature. A single glass sphere, or marble, of 475 composition by Johns-Manville will give as much as ninety miles of continuous fiber if drawn out in the common manufacturing process. Some glasses will not make fibers as well as others, but will separate. Some of these special glasses are used to make the tiny droplets or beads for reflecting surfaces on road signs and markings. Their optical properties must be carefully controlled, however, to get the maximum concentration of reflected light.

Since they are liquid solutions, adding one bit of hot glass to another of the same composition as long as both are hot enough to move poses no more problem than adding one cup of water to a pailful. Joining two different glasses to one another does pose more complicated problems. A simple test can be made to establish their compatibility. First, two small gathers taken on separate thin rods are joined side by side. A thin thread of the layered material is drawn out a yard or so in length and held under tension until cool. If the glasses are incompatible because they have different coefficients of expansion, the thread will curve. A slight curve can be tolerated, but any incompatibility builds in a strain which no annealing can remove. When testing soft laboratory glass and Pyrex, the two glasses are so incompatible that they make a spiral and eventually split apart.

Glass in the molten state is able to take into solution almost any material; platinum is the major exception. As a result, if a scientist wants to study a glass composition exactly, he has to melt it in a platinum crucible, as the glass will dissolve all other materials in some measure. Certain forms of alumina are difficult to dissolve and are therefore important refractory ingredients in lining furnaces for melting glass.

Checks, cords, seeds, stones, and blisters are the main ''defects'' looked for by the inspector in the glass plant. Nor does the artist wish to foist off on his patrons glass with dangerous self-destructive qualities: time bombs that the patron has to pay for.

Checks and cracks generally spread and indicate basic instability in the glass form. I could not sell such a piece knowing that it was bad to begin with—although I have seen a signed Tiffany piece with ''imperfect'' in the signature. It was very checked, but of such unusual color quality that evidently he could not bear to destroy it.

Cords can be decorative, as they embrace the form with a series of fine lines which also reveal its form. They sometimes come from the cooling surface of the glass in the furnace; a thickening skin is picked up in the gather and becomes part of the surface of the piece. Such cords are not destructive. But other cords resulting from improper and insufficient mixing and melting show up in the polariscope as brilliant lines, indicating great strain.

Seeds and blisters are bubbles in the glass, and the only difference between these defects and the ones previously mentioned, is that these will not cause the form eventually to explode or break apart. These may result from something as simple as a piece of dust incorporated into the glass, or from a fault in the gathering technique. They may ruin the artist's conception—or their presence may trigger a new direction.

Stones are foreign materials of a solid, opaque nature in the glass and are often the source of delayed cracks. They show up in the polariscope as bright spots with radial dark lines. They may also come from bad glass, badly mixed or badly melted. These crystalline lumps of undissolved material or material precipitated out of solution are destructive because of their incompatibility with the rest of the glass.

THIS VASE BY HENRY NAVARRE, A FOLLOWER OF MARINOT,
AND THE BOWL BELOW BY DOMINICK LABINO
ARE ENHANCED BY THE SEEDS AND BUBBLES IN THE GLASS.
(COURTESY OF THE ART INSTITUTE OF CHICAGO
AND DOMINICK LABINO.)

All in all, it is still up to the individual to decide, as Tiffany did, that cracked or not cracked, defective or not, a piece is worth saving. He must set his own standard, with the judicious use of the polariscope.

In the studio we have a homemade strain detector, a source of polarized light, and another polaroid film to look through. The prestressed patterns of wavy, multicolored lines in car windows or glass doors can be seen through polarized sunglasses. These stresses have been purposely added to give special strength and to make the glass shatter rather than break in the characteristic spears or radiating cracks from the point of impact. When our own glass is badly annealed we can see the strain in our ''strain finder.'' An easy way to make one would be to mount one lens of a pair of polaroid sunglasses over a flashlight and use the other to look through, holding the glass in between. Ours is a box with a small electric bulb mounted inside, covered with a sandwich of frosted glass, polarizing film, and another piece of glass. The other polarizing film we sandwich between two small squares of glass to protect it and tape the edges. A lump of unannealed glass from the cullet pile will be really brilliant because of the strains within it. It is also fun to check commercial glasses. Some are perfectly annealed and can serve as a goal, while others give an insight into built-in obsolescence.

Excellent durability and resistance to atmospheric and other natural corrosions have preserved the work of the past for as long as three thousand years. There is so much glass remaining from the classic Roman period that, though it may be fifteen hundred to nineteen hundred years old, it is still reasonably priced in the antiquities market. A great deal was produced, and much of it survived. (I would temper this by saying that there have also been relatively modern factories that have specialized in the unscrupulous production of ''Roman'' glass.) Over a long period of time, soft glasses are attacked by strong alkalies and other natural corrosives and may develop a crust of multicolored material, but this takes hundreds of years. The only material that really attacks glass is the extremely powerful hydrofluoric acid, so beautifully used by Gallé and Marinot.

We tend to equate glass with fragility, yet modern technology has toughened some glasses through heat and chemical means to approach the strength of the better aluminum alloys. But even without the specialized glasses of today, the thinnest glass has been strong enough to last. The Venetian style that dominated glassmaking in the Western world for so long was characterized by its delicate tendrils and gossamer forms. It was the very essence of preciousness and fragility. Many times the thin pieces have survived better than the thick, massive ones since the strains in the heavy pieces have made them more susceptible to breakage from quick temperature changes or ''heat shock.'' The thin ones were not thick enough to heat or cool unevenly.

Most glass is very hard and few materials will scratch it. It is harder than most metals and for this reason keeps its smooth surface. Normal use will not abrade the surface as is the case with plastic. Its hardness has been exploited in the sand-blasted, cut, and etched surface techniques.

In our ''now'' society, durability has almost ceased to be a factor. In fact, there are those advocating self-destructive art—perhaps so it will not be around long enough to embarrass the artist. Today, we have an increasing number of artists who are not concerned with how long a given form will last, but rather what impact it will have on people the first time they see it. They are concerned not with the object, but with the performance surrounding its presentation and display. This has given rise to paper sculpture that is washed down the drain after the opening of the exhibition, along with the other disposables of our society: paper napkins, dishes, cups, handkerchiefs, and dresses. This "now" art has joined the theater, with its happenings and the other phenomena, in our frenetic world. But given the fact that some of the frozen moments in glass do have value and should survive, we should then ask, "How long will it be considered art?" rather than, "How long will it last?" The ultimate in disposable glass art would be the blown bubble used in the factory to test for the presence of cords or streaks of uneven density in the glass. A gather is made and blown out as carefully as possible. Some grow to a dramatic size, but they are almost impossible to keep. They are often made to impress visitors in the glass plant and are beautiful in both their swelling growth and final meandering shape. Usually they are destroyed with a slap of the hand, and the thin pieces float to the floor, leaving a shimmering layer of flexible mica-like fragments over the floor. They have the beauty and durability of a soap bubble, but the visual image is so strong that it persists in the memory. The lacy patterns of the thread at the furnace mouth is another of those powerful visual images captured by the Dutch director Hofstra in his beautiful short film, *Glas.*

Glass is perfectly elastic in the sense that it will always return to its original shape when distorted. A very thin form can be carefully bent in the hand and return immediately to its original form. This elasticity or flexibility is not the same as that of an elastic band, which never quite returns to its original shape after having been bent and stretched. Glass is brittle in the sense that if a force bends it and exceeds its elastic limits, it will not stretch or dent to accommodate the force: the glass will crack or shatter.

Glass resists permanent deformation from compression for the same reasons it resists stretching—its near perfect elasticity. There is no bent or dented old glass. When it is finally broken, glass breaks with a characteristic shell-like fracture, the "conchoidal" fracture of the scientist. This was exploited in the obsidian tools and ornaments of pre-Columbian times. Today we have the same fracture as the basis for the sparkling "dalles" glass windows, the heavy, inch-thick glass set in concrete. To make the glass more brilliant, large chips are knocked off the edges of the glass pieces in a random fashion. In a glass, the molecules have no definite pattern and there are no cleavage planes.

The unique properties emanating from its elasticity give glass a great potential for artists interested in sound and movement. Sculptors in other media have introduced movement into their works, the most outstanding example being Alexander Calder with his mobiles. Harry Bertoia made some pieces which used both sound and movement, usually from incidental sources—they had to be touched to move and give off sound vibrations. Other sculptors are using motors and other means to introduce movement. Glass responds beautifully to movement, not only because of its elasticity but because of its smoothness and nearly friction-free surfaces. Industry has developed glass springs, utilizing the perfect resistance of glass to fatigue, to be used in special circumstances where other materials fail. The elasticity of glass may occur within rather narrow limits, but its movement is still within the possibility of exploration for the artist.

Because of its elasticity, glass resonates to sound waves and its vibrations can give off very accurate tones. In the eighteenth century, Benjamin Franklin invented the armonica, using this principle. The instrument consisted of a series of glass hemispheres of descending size mounted on a horizontal shaft with the edges of the hemispheres rotating in a pan of shallow water. It was played by touching the rims of the glasses. Mozart composed a work, a solo adagio, for the instrument. Some of the most beautiful small bells have been composed of glass. Since sound is being used by sculptors today, to ignore the potentialities of glass seems absurd.

Glass exhibits another whole range of qualities dependent on its light transmission, absorption, and refraction, its optical properties. Glass can be made to absorb all light except that within a given range, transmitting only the characteristic color of that wave length. The thicker the glass, the greater the absorption and the darker the color. It can be made completely opaque, black, by absorbing all the light incident to the surface, or made white to reflect and scatter all light.

Though glass may be made as transparent as possible, it still modifies light. Glass bends or refracts light, just as water does. The curve of the side of a blown form changes the images we see through the form. The thick and thin wall from the top to bottom distorts images seen through it. The slight changes in density of the liquid itself distort the view of the other side.

The refractive qualities of glass were exploited in the past. There were cuttings that created angles of reflection, and there were cuttings that created a dispersion of the light into its colored parts, an almost prismatic effect making essentially colorless glass brilliantly colored. Finally, there were cuttings into shallow facets that created a multiplicity of images, a kaleidoscopic view through the walls of the form. Precise prismatic cutting is perhaps too much work for the possible enhancement of a form, too much of a tour de force. However, some of the simplest cutting of edges and flat cuts exploit the optical properties of glass. A flattening of a curved wall by grinding and polishing a small surface gives the effect of a concave lens. Recently I have exploited the refractive brilliance of simple blown hemispheres by cutting and polishing the edges. The cut surface lets you see into the wall of the hemisphere, and the light is concentrated by the curving sides and reflected back out the cut edge. This gives a rich, deep, intense colored circle of light.

The artist can accept these qualities of glass as limitations or he can exploit them. A wall can be made thick and thin while working with the hot glass by adding hotter glass to the surface of harder glass underneath, or with the old optic mold. In fact, one technique can cancel another—a complicated optic mold was often used to hide some of the cordiness or other defects. An optic mold was usually a single cast metal form with a ribbed inside or a two-part mold with a diamond pattern of raised lines on the inside surface. A very hard cold sphere with another gather of hot soft glass over it was shoved quickly into the mold before the hot glass had softened the inner wall. This resulted in a thick and thin wall section that retained the disparity of thickness and the pattern as it was expanded into the final form. The distortion of images seen through the wall gave rise to the name "optic mold."

Capturing the transient qualities of glass is the challenge of the material. A month, a year, or centuries are not as important as the enrichment, the reinforcing, the doubling of the impact of a new vision. All of these physical and chemical properties are ordinary to the glassworker. Making them apparent to the public will suffice for the present, but the artist must penetrate beyond what is commonplace to create new form statements from qualities inherent in the material.

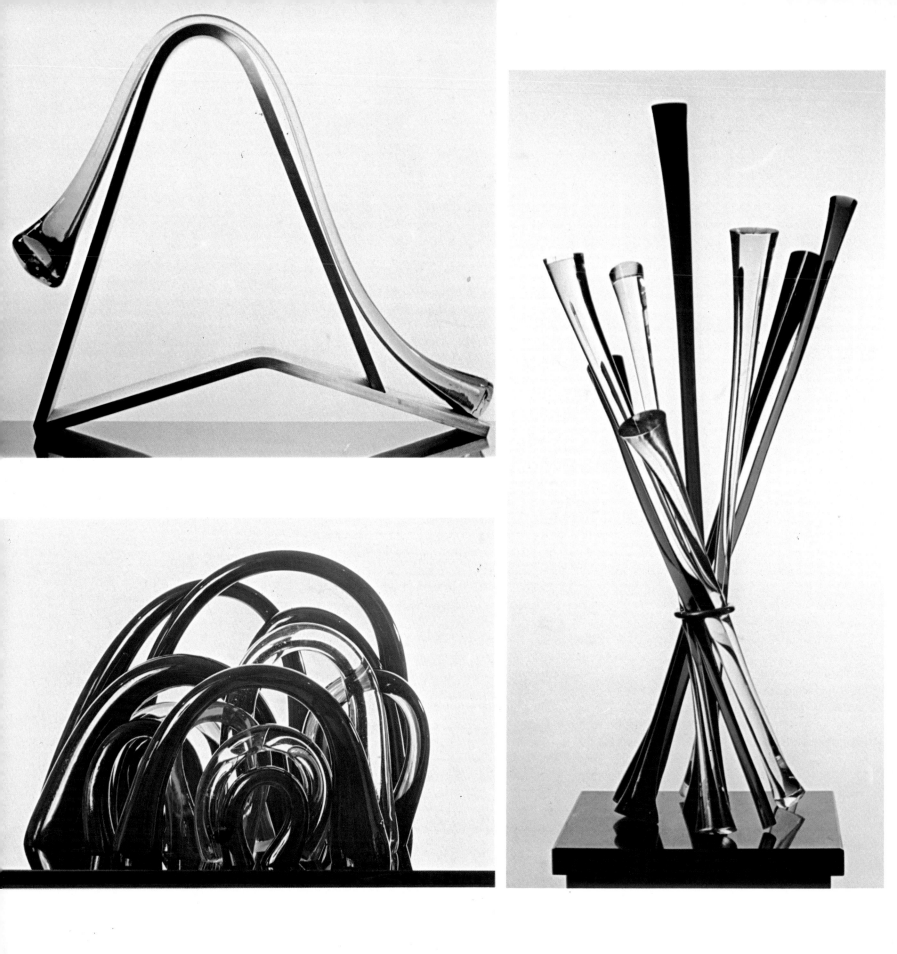

4 The Composition of Glass

The most important thing to remember about glass is that its physical properties are affected by changes in composition. When we speak of batch or a batch melt, we are speaking of mixtures of the inorganic powders either before or after melting.

Brill's article in the *Journal of Glass Studies* concerns itself with the specific compositions of glass only theoretically. We must be concerned with composition on a practical basis. Can we get the required temperature to melt a batch of glass? Can we control its quality? Will we be able to hold it in a molten state for a sufficient time? Will we be able to vary its color? Can the colors be made compatible? Can we cut and polish the finished glass?

The first requisite in a glass is that it not be subject to devitrification under normal conditions. Glasses which meet this requirement show a large variation in composition. Most glassware contains silica as its dominant component, although there are some silica-free glasses. Silica glasses possess the important quality of superior resistance to weathering, and silica is the cheapest of the glass-forming materials. Pure silica fused into a glass possesses in the highest degree the desirable qualities of freedom from devitrification and resistance to weathering. If it were not so difficult to melt, to fine—to rid of bubbles—and to work, it would be most suitable for the majority of glass uses. Other oxides must be added to lower the melting point, to decrease the viscosity, and to achieve a workable temperature range. In addition, there are some uses of glass in which the modification of the properties of silica obtained by the incorporation of other oxides is essential. Lead and other heavy metals increase the refractive index and make it softer. Lime makes it set up faster. The art of the glass smelter lies chiefly in the choice and proportioning of the ingredients according to the qualities desired in the finished glass.

The most generally used type of glass is soda-lime glass, in which the modifier of the silica is a source of sodium oxide, usually soda ash, made stable with the addition of some source of calcium oxide, usually limestone. There are usually additions of magnesia, alumina, and boron oxide of the order of one percent or so to increase the chemical stability, to aid in fining, to increase or decrease the working range. Increasing the amounts of these materials at the expense of the alkalies—the soda or potassium—results finally in the type of glasses known as the borosilicates, the ''pyrex'' heat-resistant, low-expansion glasses used for cooking and laboratory ware.

Another important group of glasses is the lead crystals. ''Crystal'' is a misnomer. Technically, a crystal and a glass are opposites, but the name arose from cut quartz crystals. There are in our museums vessels made from single quartz crystals dating as early as dynastic Egypt. By the sixteenth century, Bohemians, who were adept at this cutting, searched out an easier material to cut, coming up with a soft glass which started the cut-glass craze that dominated glass design until the colored glass of the Victorian era. Today when we speak of ''crystal'' or ''crystal glass'' this is generally what is meant.

These lead glasses substitute lead oxide for lime. They are used in tableware and also in lenses. As the lead is increased in the formula, potassium oxide replaces the sodium.

There are many other and overlapping types of glasses, but roughly the main types would be the soda-limes, potash-leads, borosilicates, and fused quartz. There are special glasses with no quartz, others with no lime, and others with large additions of barium. However, an artist need not know all about every one or, for that matter, more than one.

Opposite—
Top left:
''SYMPATHETIC MOVEMENT,''
FURNACE-WORKED FORM OF SELENIUM GLASS
WITH ALUMINUM , BY THE AUTHOR, 1970.

Bottom left:
''OPPORTUNITY TRAP,''
BLOWN-GLASS RODS, FURNACE-WORKED,
BY THE AUTHOR, 1970.

Right:
''4, 5, 6, PICK UP STICKS,''
BLOWN-GLASS RODS, FURNACE-WORKED,
BY THE AUTHOR, 1970.

The soda-lime-silica glasses were generally called "crown" and the lead-based glasses were called "flints," but these terms have more or less been discarded in favor of the more accurate designation of a glass in terms of its most important modifiers of the silica. We speak of soda-lime, potash-lime, lead or potash-lead, borosilicate, barium glass. We also commonly speak of glass according to its use, such as "window glass," "sheet glass," "flat" or "plate glass," "bottle glass," "laboratory glass"—which is either "hard" or "soft"—and "stemware." A great many names grow out of usage in a particular factory. Pyrex was the original trade name for the Corning Glass Works' borosilicate glass, and is now known generally the world over. Numbers are also used in many factories for particular glasses. The number used to identify the 96 percent silica glass at Corning when I was there was 790, and everyone knew what it was, just as now many of us in studio glassblowing are using 475 glass in the form of marbles from the Johns-Manville Glass Fibers Division. The 475 marbles are a low-temperature borosilicate glass. It was the first fired workable cullet available in quantity for glassworking in the schools. In fact, in the first year of our program at Wisconsin it was donated by the company.

The coloration of glass is relatively simple in comparison to coloring glaze or enamel, since the glass is much thicker and so little color is needed. A test of color is just a matter of sticking a thin steel rod into the molten batch and pulling out a bit to cool and look at. In testing ceramic glaze one must normally wait several days to learn the results of any changes.

Color is introduced into glass by the addition of small amounts of metallic oxides such as copper, silver, cobalt, manganese, iron, and nickel. Color is both the easiest and most complex problem of glass melting. It is so easy, as I did in the beginning, to sprinkle a little copper carbonate on a shovelful of marbles and throw them into the furnace. If the color was too strong when the marbles were melted down a few hours later, I would throw in more marbles to dilute it. If it was too weak, I would throw in more marbles with copper carbonate; what could be simpler! I used the carbonates instead of oxides because I got a little more stirring action from the carbon dioxide coming off after the surface was fused over. Cobalt goes in as easily, though I used powder blue because the oxide or carbonate is so strong a coloring agent.

Color develops in the glass in a variety of ways. The coloring oxide can disperse in the solution as a dye disperses in water, moving quickly with the convection currents and the stirring action of escaping gases throughout to give the glass an even color. The colorant can be dispersed throughout the liquid in the same way but still remain as opaque particles reflecting their characteristic color, in colloidal suspension.

The most dramatic development of color is "striking." Striking is the appearance of color after cooling and reheating, and it occurs when the coloring oxide is dissolved and precipitates out of solution as a colloidal suspension. The usual method of striking a color in glass is to cool it on the pipe or punty and to bring out the color by reheating it in the glory hole. Reduced copper in small quantities, aided by iron and tin, strikes to give beautiful copper reds. When reds are used, there often seems to be too little color, and this situation is often the most intriguing because the glass will not show red—if copper is used—until it has cooled and been reheated either in working or by re-annealing.

Selenium, which gives browns to reds, is often used to counter the iron-green color characteristic of most colorless glass produced today. The iron is not intentionally added, of course, but comes from impurities in the raw materials, and in larger quantities gives delightful colors. Selenium is quite a powerful coloring agent, and it requires only a minute amount to decolorize a batch. A small penknife-blade-full will often clear up two hundred pounds of batch that otherwise would have had a greenish look.

Glass decolorized with tiny quantities of cobalt and selenium comes out quite well. That is, the pieces come out quite colorless when I make them in a very direct manner and do not reheat them much. But selenium strikes more and more, depending on the amount of time spent in the subsequent reheating. Thus, if you want colorless glass, it might be better to use another decolorizer, or to use such pure materials that no iron is introduced. Best, of course, is to develop a philosophical approach to glass that lets you accept the glass that you melt with all its supposed defects. Then you may create your aesthetic after the melting process is completed.

Color becomes a difficult thing for the glass artist when he wants several colors in the same piece, or unusual colors, or precise control of color. These procedures involve calculation, measurement, and precision. Dominick Labino, who is a great master of color and composition in glasses, says that the best published reference on such techniques is Woldermar Weyl's *Coloured Glasses,* the second edition published in London in 1959. The January Ceramic Materials Issue of *Ceramic Industry* magazine treats colorants for glass quite extensively.

I have worked more in response to whatever color I achieved at the moment, enjoying the more unpredictable colorants like silver, with its myriad day-to-day changes than the completely predictable colors such as cobalt. I think it is fair to say that coloring is so easy that anyone can do it; once he has done it, he will study its more complex possibilities. There are few secrets today and there is almost an excess of information, so that any attempt to do a penetrating study here would be not only redundant but out of place.

One of the little-recognized properties of glass is that it resoftens at a lower temperature than the one necessary to get the materials in solution originally. The implication is that it is cheaper to remelt a glass than it is to make an original melt. However, glass remelted several times loses some of its working qualities. Lime characteristically shortens the ''setting up'' time, the time it takes the fluid glass coming from the furnace to cool or set so that the form becomes fixed. The artist wants as long a working range as possible. Throw-away bottles, on the other hand, have a short setting up time to allow for faster production. S. R. Scholes, in his *Modern Glass Practice,* says that previously melted glass or cullet of the same composition is normally added to a batch to make melting easier; but it is not necessary. Dominick Labino prefers to use a new batch every time, as he says there is more brilliance and easier color control. Good working properties may be necessary, although some artists have responded to more obdurate materials from industry where 50 percent cullet has been added to the batch, but the artist will not generally make such great demands on the material that he will need to make his own batch if a good supply of workable, remeltable glass is available. This is the reason that we at the University of

Wisconsin decided to work with cullet. I have found that some of the compositions I recently melted cost twice as much per pound as the cullet I was using. In the end, the composition will be decided by the standards an artist sets for himself, which are always intensely personal.

Another reason for using cullet is that it gives off noxious fumes to a lesser degree than does melting batch. In either case, however, a good hood is necessary for good ventilation, and both teacher and student should be made aware of this hazard.

Any attempt to be too exact in compounding a batch is usually frustrated by the fact that the raw materials rated of industrial grade are not pure. Some sands are contaminated with iron or clay. Dolomitic limestone has a relative ratio of calcium to magnesium, but varies as to its source and impurities (generally iron and alumina). These variations can be controlled in a factory, but the artist must use the trial-and-error method or accept a material already melted and somewhat standardized. Here it is also my experience from using 475 marbles for a period of five years that different shipments are not always the same nor are they always compatible. Once I realized this I was careful not to mix material from different shipments, but I had lost several days' work before this became apparent.

I believe that the melting of batch formulas has great potential for the artist; however, I do not believe it is primary to the development of a form-sense in glass.

In my first five years of work with glass, I used cullet and was able to achieve a wide range of color and form. The excitement I now feel with the glasses I am melting in no way detracts from the validity of that previous work. Being forced by my background to recapitulate in the studio those techniques I had known in the factory, I found this an easier transference using cullet. The speed with which I and all the young people in this country have developed through these initial stages is proof of the efficiency of cullet in a beginning situation.

The chart on page127 gives a series of batch compositions equally weighed out. It must be understood that the weights are not the actual amounts of any one ingredient present in the *melted* glass because of the losses and chemical changes that take place in melting. To get a batch formula for a composition, one has to make educated guesses as to the loss of gases and the necessary choice of materials to produce the final ingredients. Natural materials have impurities and variations. Such calculations are beyond the scope of the beginner and of little import to the artist. It is not, however, difficult to make adjustments in a given batch formula within the limits of that type of glass. This is a matter of trial and error, that fabled activity of the white-collar scientist which he calls the empirical approach when his theoretical calculations fail.

There are many published batch formulas for good workable glasses available. The problem is never the initial formula but adapting it to your own conditions and materials. It is true that the artist reacts to the material, and in this case *any* glass can have special virtue, if we know how to make the most of it. Dr. Donald Stookey, a research scientist in the Corning Glass Works Laboratory, had been working with a white photosensitive glass which was overheated one day, and in throwing it out he found it very hard to break; in fact, aside from its other wonderful properties, it was almost unbreakable. He had, of course, been concerned all along about the nature of the changes in the basic structure of the glass and was highly sensitive to anything out of the ordinary. The result was the unique material that Corning Glass Works called Pyroceram, a crystalline nonmetal with amazing strength and heat resistance.

At the same time, since the artist wants no limitations on his material, he should realize that he can adapt and change a glass to make more of whatever he finds he enjoys in the glass, but he should not waste his time in experimentation *for its own sake.*

Once anyone has gone through an intensive period of a month or so melting a glass and observing its properties, I believe he has the understanding needed to exploit that particular glass as a medium of his own expression.

5 Tools

Some artists must have every tool that was ever made, while others want only a few. Yet, with all the tools I have accumulated, every time I read about or visit a new locality or factory, I see more. I cannot catalog them all here. In essence, this section will serve as a glossary of the traditional usage of tools, and will include some personal commentary on their multiplicity of uses in solutions to problems as well as their implications for form statement.

Blowpipes

A blowpipe is a hollow tube usually 48″ to 52″ long with a tapered end. It is made of mild steel about ⅝″ OD with a ⅛″ wall. The end is about ⅞″ OD, tapering back about 2″ to the tube. The blowpipe comes in all sizes, depending on the height of the worker and his strength. It is not necessarily so that the bigger the pipe, the larger the piece you can make with it. In some factories a very large end was used for making tumblers because the right amount of glass could be gathered the first time and the production time was cut. In Germany a smaller pipe is used for large forms because the end cools the glass less and the piece does not cool so quickly. A heavier pipe may be necessary to counterbalance a heavy piece, but one can also cool the pipe so that the hands can be held farther apart, giving more mechanical advantage over the piece at the end. In working out of a smaller furnace the pipe need not be so long. Pipes made in Germany by the Putsch Company are stocked by the Paoli Clay Company of Route 1, Belleville, Wisconsin.

Punties

A punty is a solid rod for gathering glass. It is used after the blowing is finished: the punty is attached to the base of the piece so that the neck, or opening where the piece is broken off the blowpipe, can be finished by reheating and shaping. The punty is about ⅜″ to ½″ in diameter and is usually made of mild, cold rolled steel with a stainless tip. Sometimes it is easier just to buy a length of stainless steel and grind the tip. The punty is, of course, about the same length as the blowpipe. I also like to have a couple of small punties about ³/₁₆″ to ¼″ in diameter to gather small bits.

Yokes

The yoke is a Y-shaped support for the blowpipe. In Sweden I purchased one with two steel balls in the corners of a cast U-shaped piece. The balls are set in a hole slightly larger than they are so that they can roll freely on small ball bearings underneath. This yoke has some advantages, but in the Eisch factory it was discarded for a simple bent rod welded onto an upright. I have several yokes in my studio so that I can go from furnace to glory hole or work standing up in the German manner, using the yoke as a support.

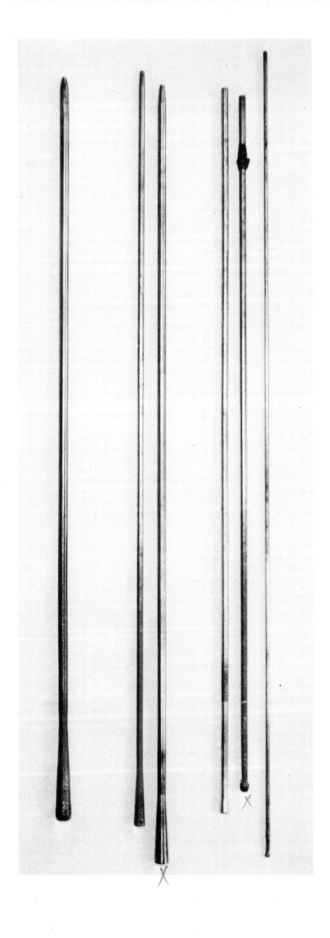

Benches

A simple bench, extended to the right for right-handed people (this is one of those flagrant examples of prejudice pointed out by the National Association for the Advancement of Left-Handed People!), has two arms extending forward to support a blowpipe as it is rolled back and forth to work the glass form. A shield is customarily dropped from the right side to protect the worker's legs from the radiant heat. The bench extension holds the jacks, shears, and other small tools. Water buckets with the wood tools are customarily just behind this bench extension but within reach of the outstretched hand of the seated worker.

It is easy to build your own bench. In October 1963 when I gave a workshop for the Ohio Designer-Craftsmen at the workshop of Dominick Labino, we built one in a short time. However, we did not get the seat very high because the scraps we used were too short. Labino used this bench for some years and he objects to my benches as being "too high."

Furnaces

Furnaces are of two types: pots and tanks. In a pot furnace the glass is in a refractory container or clay pot; in the tank, the bottom of the furnace itself holds the glass.

In my earliest experiments I quickly ruled out pot melting with commercial pots as too expensive and too complicated for a beginner: I broke all I tried. I was successful using a few of my own thrown-stoneware pots for short working cycles of two or three days, but there was a great problem in cleaning the furnaces once the pots were broken. One of my students has used thrown pots, too often a new pot each time, in a high school project. We have used such pots as long as four months. However, it seems to have worked out for most of us to use small "day tanks," furnaces that are charged each day. Dr. Robert Fritz at San Jose State College in California has worked out a miniature continuous tank with separate burners on two parts with a bridge wall dividing the tank, so that glass cullet can be fed in one end and melted glass can flow under the bridge wall and out the other end. Most of us use top burners for ease of construction and flexibility. Our basic purpose has been to keep the original and replacement costs at a minimum, consistent with our individual operations. Everyone involved has made his own improvements, and I cannot recommend any special type, anymore than I can say how high the door should be from the floor. I *can* say that the type of furnace and its details does eventually have some relationship to the forms produced—perhaps only so much glass can be gathered inside and any piece over a certain size will get stuck to the wall or will have small points on the side where it stuck and was pulled away.

Making a furnace is not difficult, since all bricks are standard sizes, the basic unit being 9″ x 4½″ x 2½″. By counting the bricks in the photographs it is very easy to duplicate one of my furnaces. No mortar is required, because the glass flows out the cracks and seals the furnace together as it comes into the cooler parts of the walls. I do use tie rods to bind it together in the construction and to hold it together in the expansion and contraction of successive firings.

Opposite—
Top left:
GLASSWORKER'S BENCH.
Top right:
FURNACES IN THE AUTHOR'S STUDIO.
THE GLORY HOLE, FOR REHEATING GLASS
DURING WORKING AND BEFORE ANNEALING,
IS AT THE RIGHT.
Bottom left and right:
A SMALL FURNACE IN CONSTRUCTION.

Burners

Burners for our small furnaces are quite different from those used in the industrial furnaces. The almost universal availability of natural gas and liquified petroleum fuels such as propane and butane have greatly simplified the artist's problems. Depending on the size of the furnace, the melting temperature needed, and the working cycle, I use commercially available weed burners or auxiliary heating torches like the North American blowtorch #170. For a furnace of the type illustrated, a burner delivering up to 100,000 BTUs and adjustable for oxidizing and reducing conditions will be quite suitable. A good burner for propane may be purchased from the Johnson Company of Cedar Rapids, Iowa.

Hoods

Dominick Labino's solution for a hood is the best I have seen. He has dropped a wall from the roof down to the top of the furnaces and has used a window opening with a quiet 36″ exhaust fan to clear the air. The adjustments for the burners are on the front edge of the hood so that there is little need to go under the hood at any time. Further, the lower edge is heavy enough so that he can hang shields or screens from it to raise the efficiency of the fans and to shield himself from the glare of the furnace. The glare of the furnace can be a problem, especially if one's eyes are sensitive to light. It is wise to acquire a pair of didymium glasses such as those worn by lampworkers. They are available from Bethlehem Appa-ratus Company, Bethlehem, Pennsylvania.

The illustration is of the hood in my own studio which uses an exhaust fan in the stack.

Annealing Ovens

My annealing oven is an oblong, galvanized, twenty-gauge steel box lined with two inches of 1700° block insulation and faced with one-inch alumina-silicate fiber. It is heated with two 10-ampere nickel-chromium heating elements connected to a timing device to turn it off. A second timer connected to the "on-off" timer controls a variable voltage transformer with a cam, lowering the temperature by varying the voltage from 110 to 0 volts in a period of time set when the oven is fully loaded.

The fiber under the trade name "Fiberfrax" is available from the Carborundum Corporation, Niagara Falls, New York.

The oven as illustrated does not have the fiber blanket; when it was added, the oven's efficiency was greatly increased.

Above left:
BURNER MADE BY THE AUTHOR
TO A DESIGN BY DOMINICK LABINO.
Above right:
BURNER IN PLACE IN BURNER BLOCK.

Opposite—
Top:
HOOD IN AUTHOR'S STUDIO.
Bottom left:
ANNEALING OVEN INTERIOR.
Bottom right:
CONTROL FOR AN ANNEALING OVEN.

SCULPTURES MADE WITH GLASS AND
MOLDS FOR GLASS. (COURTESY OF N. V.
KONINKLIJKE NEDERLANDSCHE GLASFABRIEK
"LEERDAM.")

Molds

The traditional wooden mold can still be found in use today in small factories. Steel, cast-iron, brass, and aluminum have also been used. The mold is water-cooled and a semipermanent mold other than wood must be coated with carbon to make for easy separation. In any but the simplest shapes, one needs small holes for the steam to escape so that pressure will not build up in any pocket.

Molds and mold blowing have various possible uses for the artist. In 1962 I was struck by the sight of Erwin Eisch using a simple box mold in the early stages of making a form. He withdrew the shape from the mold before the shape was set, and expanded and worked the shape, retaining in time only a vestige of the mold. A square mold does give a different distribution of a glass thickness in the walls than does the flattening of a shape on the marver or with a wooden paddle. The latter procedure would produce walls of even thickness and consequently would refract the light quite differently than the same mold-blown shape with the characteristic thin corners and thick sides. One of my students has been experimenting with more spontaneous mold materials using wet clay shapes backed with wood frames. At Leerdam in the Netherlands, Willelm Heesen has used a series of cast aluminum plates with low-relief patterns in a fixture so that the shape could be varied each time to produce a series of unique molded forms.

Opposite:
BOTTLES BY WILLEM HEESEN,
MADE FROM SPONTANEOUS ALUMINUM MOLDS.

Blocks

Blocks vary from country to country but are generally made of a dense, close-grained fruitwood. I have used applewood, wild cherry, and beech, beechwood being the wood used in the Eisch factory in Frauenau, Germany. Some of the blocks are made with the grain running vertically, and some horizontally. Some are cut from the limb so that you can use the growth rings almost as a guide to cut the block and others are cut from the quarter-sawed segments of the main trunk. None seems to be better than any other, but one develops personal preferences, usually based on available material. I have a favorite cut from the length of the limb. I cut my blocks with a large wood gouge, though I have used good lathe-turned blocks. Mine are ovoid in shape and not the perfectly spherical shape that results from lathe turning.

Marvers

The marver was originally a marble slab for rolling and chilling the glass. Today it is a smooth steel plate the size of which varies a great deal. It should be thin enough to be warmed by the glass, but still thick enough to absorb the heat emitted from the glass, allowing the glass to chill slightly. It should be large enough to take at least one revolution of the largest form you will make. Most factory marvers are small since these are not used as much as artists use them. Many factory workers wax the surface so that a piece does not roll along, but slides around in one position. This is a somewhat more difficult maneuver, and it is easier to just make your marver a little larger.

Paddles

Paddles are pieces of hardwood used either wet on very hot glass or dry on colder glass to achieve many of the same things normally achieved with the marver, jacks, or other tools. Labino has a series of wooden paddles with indentations of differing sizes which allow him to replace the jacks. He can draw out necks and do all of the operations normally done with other tools. As a consequence, he needs very few steel tools. The paddles burn up, but they are easily replaced.

Files

A standard, sharp, 10″ to 12″ metal file is vital on any bench to scratch the glass when breaking it off the blowpipe once the punty is fastened. Old, dull files have many uses. They are useful for knocking glass off the pipes. Often an experienced glassworker will clean a pipe by sticking it in water to crack the glass off the pipes. A word of caution, however: he always holds his finger over the mouth end to prevent the steam and hot water from being blown up the pipe and into his face! I have seen bad burns when someone forgot.

A file with edges dulled by scratching glass may be resharpened by running the thin side of the surface along an emery wheel, provided that the teeth on the flat surface have not been dulled.

Shears

Shears are of two types: trimming shears and square shears. The trimming shears are just like small tin snips of the simplest style except that the cutting edges are sharp. A tin snip has a flat edge on the blade which chills too much of the glass. If one uses them, the thicker edges of the tin shears should be filed thinner, and they will then make good shears.

The cut-off shears (square shears) used for cutting a rod or gob of glass are quite different. They have a square opening and have thin shearing edges, cutting from all four sides as they close. It is hard to improvise these, although I have seen some made by grinding a half-circle indentation on each blade of a broad-bladed tin snips, but they do not close so well. Glass cut-off shears are filed in such a manner that only the cutting edges in contact with the glass touch one another. There are several European firms that manufacture them, and Putsch shears are imported and stocked by the Paoli Clay Company.

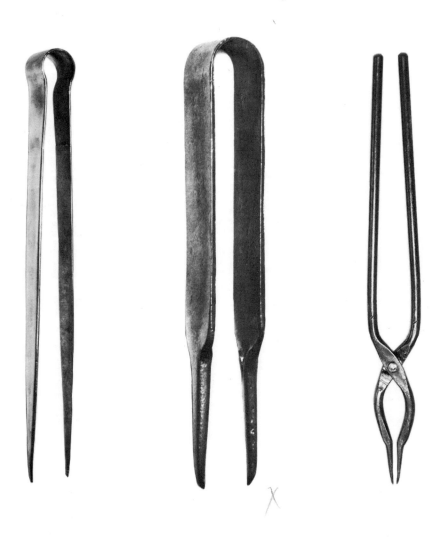

Tweezers—"Italian Tools"

In Sweden, the glassworker's outsize tweezers (and it is just that—about 10″ to 12″ long) is called the Italian tool. This is because the soft soda glass used in Murano remains workable over such a long time that the glassblowers, with the help of these tweezers, are able to pinch and pull it into wonderfully complex shapes.

The manipulation of small additions may require a kind of extension of the fingers to get in and pinch or twist that the tweezers cannot quite manage. A simple answer is small pinchers, easily made of ³⁄₁₆″ or ¼″ rod. These are used in Germany to twist and fasten handles on ceremonial goblets or small pitchers. Square shears often have an extension on the end for grasping a punty to guide it onto the form. These scissor-like ends are often used to guide the end of the handle onto the form, and the handle is then pulled out and cut off. But the shears are a little clumsy, and it may be easier to drop them and manipulate the pinchers as they do in Germany. Of course, you may not be interested in appendages, but if you have the tools available, you will eventually use them.

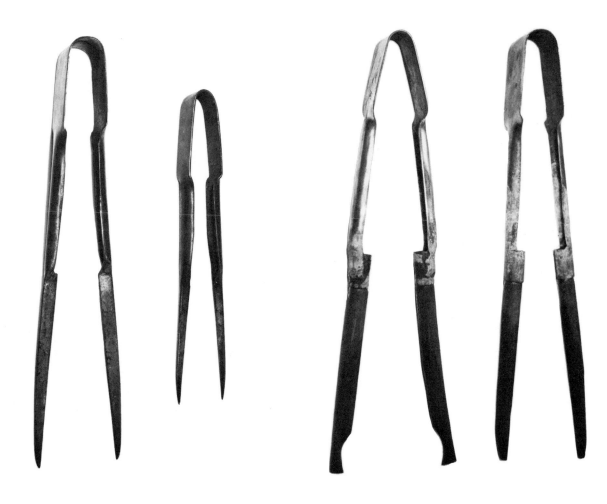

Jacks or "Pucellas"

Jacks are spring tools consisting of two long steel or wooden fingers extending downward when grasped in the hand; they are used to indent, stretch out, and otherwise form the glass. As I describe the use of the tool, however, I realize that for me the uses are endless and depend on how I feel at the moment I grab it. There is a beautiful shot of Maurice Marinot in his film, *Un Grand Verrier,* grabbing a jack and using the spring loop at the end to move the top soft glass of a last gather along the form to make a trough along the length, terminating in a knob just under the top rim.

Jacks have a wax charcoal coating to keep them from marking the glass. The coating formulas vary from worker to worker. In Germany a mixture of heavy oil and wood soot is used. In America I have seen workers use chipped beeswax or carnauba wax. A new jack is always rough and may not even be shaped. It requires quite a bit of filing and sanding to make it a tool one can really enjoy using. Wood jacks have wet wood ends made of hard fruitwood, like paddles and blocks. They burn and char so that they mark the glass very little. When they are dry the ends slip out easily for replacement. New ones can be prepared by fitting them loosely and allowing them to swell to a tight fit in water behind your bench. This keeps them ready and easily accessible. Readymade jacks can be purchased from the Paoli Clay Company.

Hooks, Ice Picks, Etc.

I have two old-style ice picks, one with the end bent into a sharp hook for making peacock-feather forms and other designs made by moving applied threads of glass up or down or around on the surface of the glass. The other is straight and is mainly for putting air bubbles into a gather where the effect is desired.

Some tools have no traditional names. I made a V-shaped dipper with a series of holes along the base of the V. It is used to cool the pipe.

There are a great number of specialized small tools for making special shapes. There are clappers of different kinds for making feet; small blocks for stem shapes; jacks for pulling out stems. I am sure that there are many others for similar jobs that I have not yet seen. I have tried some of these specialized tools, but have not found them to be any magical answer in developing a complex shape or in producing a new form.

Left:
GRINDING WHEEL IN AUTHOR'S STUDIO.
BANDING WHEEL AT THE LEFT
IS USED TO CHECK THE ACCURACY OF THE CUTTING.

Opposite—
Top:
AUTHENTIC COPPER WHEEL
ENGRAVING LATHE IN AUTHOR'S STUDIO.
Bottom:
TURNER MACHINE COMPANY
GLASSCUTTING LATHE MADE IN ENGLAND.

Cutting Equipment

Cutting is a large area, and only a few of us in America are beginning to get into it. Grinding and finishing the bases of pieces require nothing more than a hard flat surface, carborundum dust, a little water, and patience. More luxurious is a flat grinding wheel like a potter's wheel, with wet paste of carborundum applied with a brush. For polishing one needs a cork or hard felt wheel with pumice, cerium, or rouge.

Cutting does change form and does have many implications for the artist. I have recently been enjoying the cutting open of forms with an eight-inch diamond saw, cooled with water. Following the slicing, I have to grind and polish the edges of these pieces. This exploits some of the optical properties of glass that are not seen in the rounded fire-formed edges and shapes. A wet belt sander has some uses; and a 400 belt will help to bring up the polish very quickly at the end. The belt gives a directional finish quite different from the random ground surface of the lapping wheel. A cutting lathe really does not seem to me to be a necessity, perhaps because I got along without one. Although I own and have used a lathe and an engraving lathe, I have not used either much up to this time. Belt sanders and other cutting materials may be purchased from Sommer and Maca or the Lange Machine Works, both of Chicago, Illinois.

6 Techniques

Perhaps the first thing that one learns in gathering is that the tip of the blowpipe must be a dull red heat to make the gather—if it is too cold the glass will not stick on, and the glass next to the end hole will be so chilled that one cannot start a bubble.

In the first gather I try to lay the tip on top of the glass so that the shadow of the colder tip can be seen on the surface of the glass. Barely touching the glass, I make at least one revolution into the mass. The pipe is turned more, while pulling slightly back on the pipe and winding the glass gather ahead of the tip, raising it until the thread winds up and breaks with the surface. While pulling the pipe out of the furnace, I keep turning it to overcome the force of gravity while the surface tension is evening out the gather. It is then necessary to chill the surface so that there is a skin to blow against. It can be done by rolling it on a steel slab or marvering the gob into a conical or cylindrical form. If the marver is dusty there will be a layer, usually of tiny bubbles, when the next gather is made. Maurice Marinot purposely spread glass enamels, crusted glass and/or chemicals, on the marver to accomplish his colored inclusions. I was told at Boda in Sweden that they used ground manure. Hans Christian Wagner, a Danish potter who became interested in glass, designed some pieces rolled in cobalt. These inclusions, however, can "dirty" the glass and upset someone else's plans in the studio when the marver is not properly cleaned. It can also be dangerous, as the melted chemical might cause burns on contact with skin.

Pages 75 and 76

MARVERED FIRST GATHER.

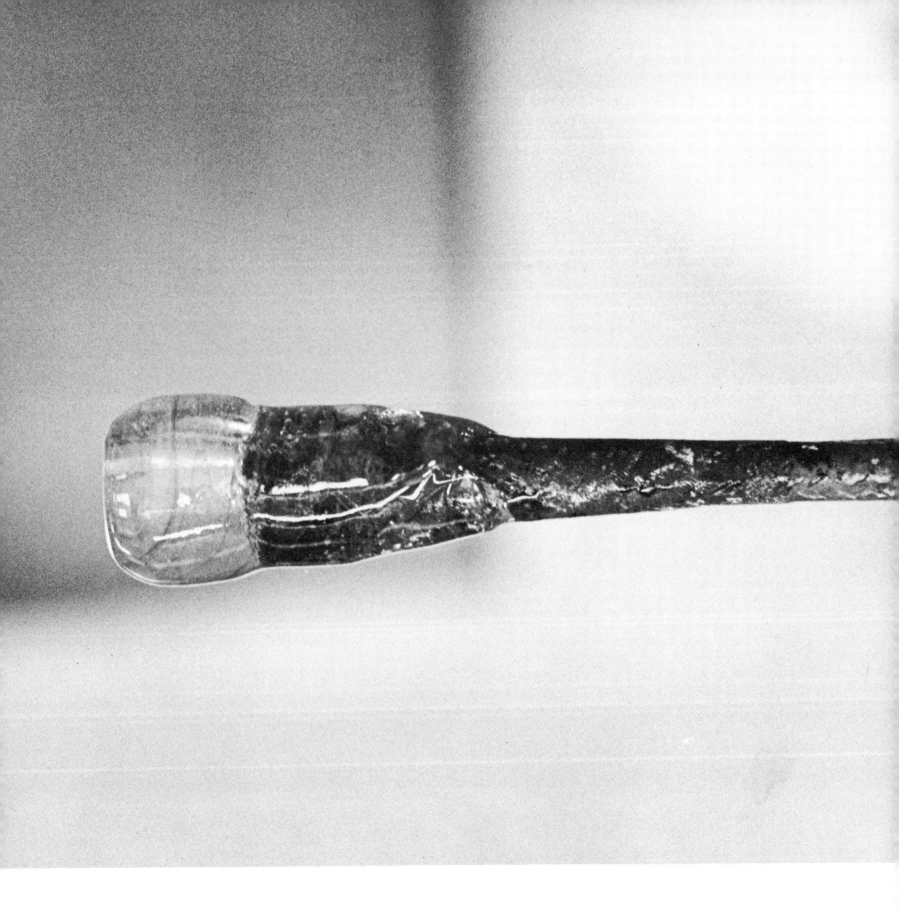

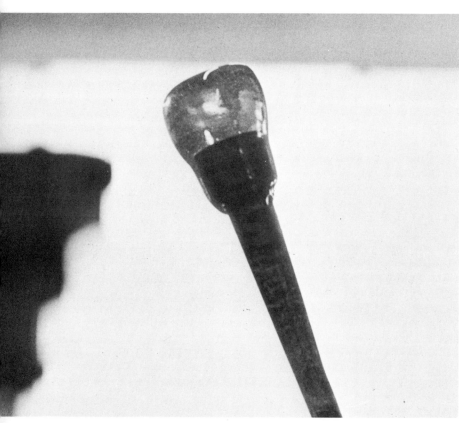

THE GATHER HELD UP AND INFLATED.

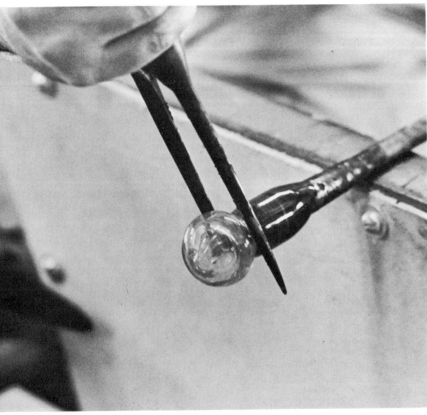

NECKING THE SPHERE.

CHILLING THE BUBBLE.

Still turning the pipe, I point it up and blow to start the bubble. As the cylindrical form fattens from sagging back on itself and the turning keeps it centered on the pipe, the bubble will pop out. I can notice this by a change in the refraction of the light and the color of the glass. Once this bubble is made, I must chill the bubble until the color is gone before another gather of glass is made. If the piece is small, it is wise to neck the sphere, or indent it with a small groove, just ahead of the pipe, making it possible to break it at the neck when you later transfer it to the punty.

GATHERING THE SECOND GATHER.

The second gather is made by driving the pipe and bubble into the hot glass with a sharp movement to prevent gathering blisters. I do not gather up to the iron this time because it would soften the neck, making the glass more difficult to control. With this gather, though it might also be done with the first instead of marvering, the glass is blocked at the bench.

Blocking, the traditional method of cooling the outer skin so that there is something to blow against, has itself given rise to a whole series of forms known as "paperweights" and "doorstops." Paperweights are seldom more than inclusions within two or more gathers which are only blocked to shape them.

BLOCKING.

Most forms of any size require a series of gathers and blocking operations, one on top of the other, to achieve a large mass of glass all under control. One step is much like the other; each gather brings proportionately more glass into the ball than all the previous gathers. With the increasingly heavy thicknesses of glass to cool and control, it is better to cool the under glass more each time, so long as it does not become so cold that it will break off.

Many forms are derived in the most direct manner from the tools and processes, especially those forms traditionally done by the workers during their breaks and brought home as gifts for friends and family.

When I return with the hot glass from the furnace to the bench, I cannot take my eyes off it. I must sit down and place the pipe on the arms of the bench and reach for the wet block, all without ceasing to watch the glass, turning the pipe to keep the gather centered and tipping the end up or down to distribute the glass and control the shape before the block slowly comes up to the ball of the glass. In blocking, the wood itself never actually touches the glass. There is a layer of superheated steam between the block and the glass, the wet carbon from the charred surface of the block preventing the glass and wood from sticking. If the block dries out too much, the glass will stick and tiny bits of carbon are often stuck to the glass, causing bubbles or dirty marks where the ash is left on the glass.

Blocking both chills and evens up the surface. It is for me a beautiful movement, light and easy, just coaxing the hot glass over the surface of the colder glass underneath to distribute it in an even layer, perhaps making the base thicker or lengthening the form. By tipping the pipe to let gravity help at this point, the glass outside is slowly cooled while the cooler glass inside is heated. It is now a lovely rosy orange color which is alive in its movement; the slightest breath in the pipe will swell out the form. If another gather is necessary, it is the same process all over again, now on a larger scale.

Above:
GATHERING THE THIRD GATHER.
Below:
BLOCKING THE THIRD GATHER.

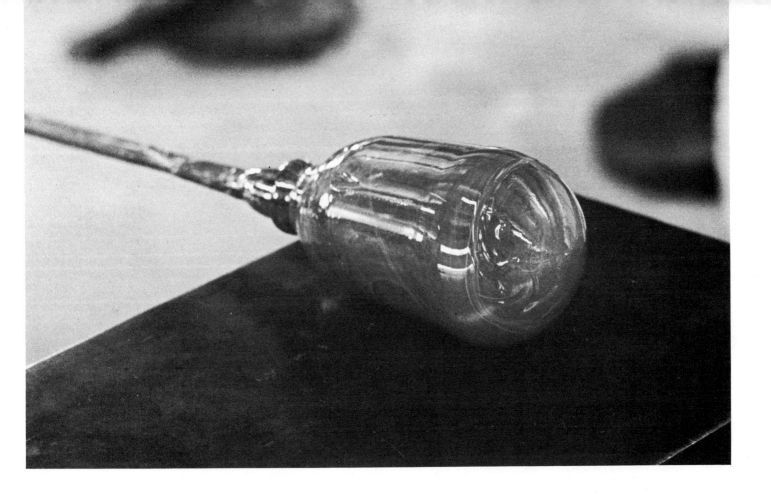

Once the gather has been made and the sphere blown out, the base can be flattened slightly for the punty. All the variations on the original sphere are generally made now: letting it be pulled into a long teardrop by gravity, or rolling it onto the marver to make it into a cylinder, flattening it with paddles, necking it with jacks or wooden tools—and reheating it from time to time to keep it workable. Here the beginner often forgets the relatively cold pipe and its attachment and loses the piece by having it crack off. It is only a little trouble to keep that part heated in the glory hole or to add a ring of hot glass over the end of the pipe. In fact, if the piece is to be finished by cutting off the ''moil'' (the extra glass next to the pipe), another ring of hot glass should be added just on the neck of the piece below the joint where the form will be broken off.

Attaching a punty or ''pontil'' to give an adequate attachment or easy break is accomplished in many different ways and indicates the many possible solutions to a single technical problem. In Germany the punty glass is rolled in sand, giving an imperfect joint. In Sweden an ''X'' is marked with chalk on the base of the piece before attaching a gob. In Italy several methods are used to indent the center of the bit gather so that only a circle of glass is attached. At other times, points are pulled out like a little crown for a very delicate attachment. In the factory when I was a boy there was a round steel plate attached to the bench with slots about 3/16'' wide and 3/16'' deep, 3/8'' apart, crisscrossing the surface; the hot punty was touched to this first before sticking up. The 3/8'' squares made chilled indentations on the bit gather and left a cross-web of hot glass for the hot attachment. Some of the gaffers first make a crosslike indentation, using the edge of the marver to make the punty attachments incomplete. Others marver the punty down to almost a point, leaving a small point of hot glass surrounded by chilled glass as it is pushed on to the base, making a less perfect joint.

ATTACHING THE PUNTY.

Once the punty is attached, a sharp wet file is used to scratch the glass where it will be broken off the blowpipe. A sharp tap on the pipe away from the piece detaches it. An easy movement of the punty and the cold neck is ready at the mouth of the furnace or the glory hole. Too quick an entry here can check, or crack, the form. At the same time, the piece must be kept turning in the yoke to keep it centered.

Steam pressure has been used for blowing or reinflating a piece on the punty. This is done either by pushing a wet stick through the narrow opening of the form or by holding the opening down over a damp surface, a wet board, or a pad of wet paper. Air pressure, from either a simple mouth-blown conical tool or an air hose, is traditionally used to inflate a form.

The conical end of such a tool fits a variety of openings, and when it is forcibly held against an opening and air pressure is applied, the form can be expanded. This process has been used both to inflate a form that has been broken from the pipe and to start a piece gathered on a punty. In 1962 Jean Sala gave me a tool similar to those I later saw used in Murano. Sala's, however, had a simple right-angle bend to make it possible for him to use it alone.

At Steuben the cone is made of wood and is on the end of an air hose with a simple finger valve so that the gaffer or head of the hand shop can use it without aid. There I saw it used to open out the top of a high bowl. After the piece was broken off the pipe and warmed in the glory hole, air pressure was used to open up that thick area of glass near the rim. Normally, such a form would be slowly opened out with the jacks and the wall would never be pulled outward from the base. But the entrapped, expanding air bubble pulled out and thinned the wall farther and farther toward the base. This is quite a different action from the stretching outward of the edge with a jack or even the spinning out of a form with centrifugal force.

MOUTH-BLOWN TOOL FOR
INFLATING GLASS ON THE PUNTY.

THE AUTHOR INFLATING GLASS ON THE PUNTY.
NOTE THAT THE LEFT HAND HOLDS THE PUNTY.
THE BEND IN THE INFLATING TOOL ALLOWS
THE ARTIST TO ACCOMPLISH THIS TASK
UNASSISTED.

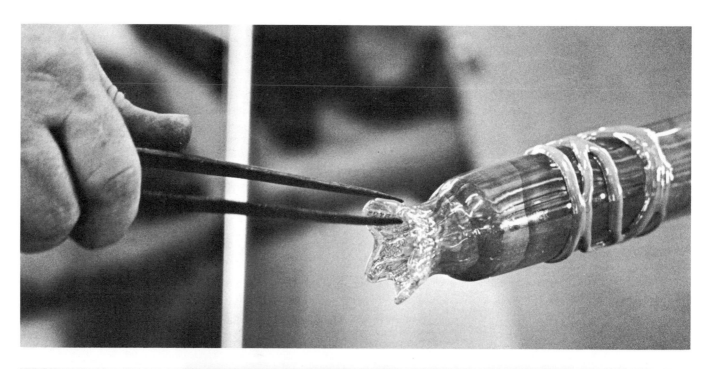

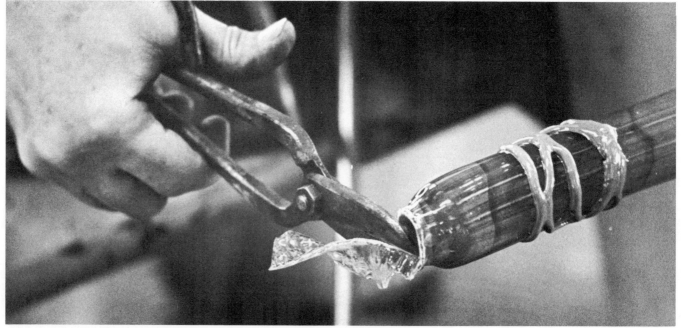

In Italy the outward pull to thin the top edge is often done by pulling it out little by little with the tweezers, making a crownlike edge which is trimmed off. This gives a controlled, open, tapering wall similar to and in some ways better than that achieved by blowing it out. It is possible to preplan the distribution of the glass in the wall of the original bubble before it is opened out to control wall thickness. But the normal tendency is to work with the wall thickness that results naturally from the process.

To finish the neck, a sharp flame is necessary on the lip and a gentler heat on the body of the piece. In industry, the glory hole is a large roaring monster with up to six mouths spurting flames out at the workers skulking behind their shields. The men are concentrating on the exact moment when the neck will be soft enough without deforming the main body of the form. Depending on the size of the neck, a series of refractory rings is used around the opening to the glory hole to get the spurt of the flame the right size. The extra flame envelops the form softly to keep the piece warm.

For smaller pieces that easily fit the door opening, I do most of the reheating in the furnace with the top burner designed by Dominick Labino. For larger pieces, I use the glory hole. Mine is a thirty-gallon steel drum lined with quartz or alumina silicate fiber and heated by a similar top burner. To narrow the opening of this reheating furnace I have also used a ring made of sheet metal and backed by fiber insulation.

The termination, the lip, the mouth, and the neck of the piece are formed on reheating. (I am always amazed that we give these things such human terms, and of course many artists have followed by making any opening parallel to the openings of the human body. Bernard Leach has a wonderful section in his *A Potter's Book* that concerns the openings of pottery forms and their similarity to the mouth. Our young artists have pushed these concepts much farther in the abstractions of today. Anthropomorphic forms develop so easily in glass.) A wooden stick or the doubled ends of the jack are used to flare out the glass to make the opening as the piece is rolled on the arms of the bench. If the traditional top rim is desired, the jacks make an indentation just behind the lip, working against the glass already chilled by the flaring tool. Now is the time to make the characteristic bottle neck by pulling outward on the jack to stretch the neck. The angle of the lip has to be determined before the neck is formed, because, if the neck is to have any length, the lip cannot be reheated after stretching the neck without softening the neck, causing the artist to lose control of it. Many thin narrow necks have heavy top rims because the lip was not made thin enough before stretching.

A small stopper is made in much the same manner by jacking in a small bubble on the pipe or a solid ball on the punty and pulling outward. A number of interesting closed forms with knoblike terminations have come out of the student work with these extended necks.

In making a long neck, elongation of the form can more easily take place on the punty than on the blowpipe, after the forming operations are almost complete. The distance from the cool end of the punty to the end of the elongated glass form becomes too great to finish the lip. It seems best to stretch the neck just before breaking the piece off into the annealing oven.

Flattening surfaces on the marver can also be accomplished while the piece is on the punty, but care is needed that the piece is hot enough to prevent surface checks or tiny cracks resulting from contact with the cool surface of the marver. Often it is better to use a dry wooden paddle since it burns with any

THE GLORY HOLE.

prolonged contact with the glass and provides a much less drastic chilling. Besides, if you are demonstrating, a little smoke and flame are very dramatic. Some exciting changes can occur by applying force not only on the outside of the form but from the inside as well. If the piece is rotated, pressure from a stick results in a raised line or ridge around the form. If the glass is soft, the area affected is quite localized, but when the glass is harder, more of the wall is distorted (there is an old adage among glassworkers: Don't get too stiff!).

A bowl can be spun open by rolling the punty down the arm, using centrifugal force. Whenever the walls are not of an even thickness, there will be an irregular edge. Low forms with great outstretched projections are made by adding glass to areas on the sides and spinning the form out, the extra glass moving at an increased rate as its weight distorts the form and pulls outward.

A last gentle reheating helps in the annealing by evening out the strain of the working at this point. Difficult annealing problems are often solved by heating the piece above the softening point in the glory hole and then bringing the temperature down more evenly in the annealing oven. The hotter it goes into the annealing oven the better, as long as it does not change shape. I have seen factory workers holding complicated pieces at the end of the lehr (a long narrow annealing chamber) with a small fire of sticks and newspapers to try to achieve this heating before the piece is cracked off the punty. Some glasses break cleanly when the piece is taken off the punty for annealing. A sharp blow on the punty away from the piece seems to do a good job. At other times, a nick on the joint with a sharp point, followed by short taps on the punty away from the piece, will break it away.

It is reasonable to assume that in annealing, the lower the temperature in relation to the top of the annealing range, the longer the piece will have to soak to even out the strain. Annealing is an empirical process; any attempt by the artist, who is making a series of different forms of differing thicknesses and in shapes he has never seen before, to calculate annealing time by a formula is practically impossible.

The simplest test to determine the annealing temperature of any glass is to heat it until it bends and then anneal it at about fifty degrees or so below that temperature. If there are too many strains, raise the temperature slightly or lengthen the annealing time. To be more exact, a standard test can be devised by taking an 8″ glass rod of ¼″ diameter and placing it in the annealing oven with the ends resting on two bricks. When the glass sags, the annealing temperature for that glass should be about 50°F. below this temperature. Most glasses anneal between 800°F. and 1100°F., depending on their composition.

Once a piece is out of the annealing oven, it should be inspected for strain. Through a process of trial and error, the artist's experience with the same equipment and a particular glass should allow him to estimate competently the proper annealing temperatures and the necessary time.

In Italy, in the small factories of Murano, a lehr is often built alongside the furnace to utilize the exhaust flame and gases from the glass melting. The end nearest the furnace has an opening with an asbestos curtain or a sheet-iron door. Here the temperature is tested by putting in crumpled newspaper and counting the seconds needed for it to ignite. The heat can be controlled by a damper. The newly made pieces are placed in the chamber with a long-handled wooden paddle and moved along periodically through the heat zones toward the cool end with a forked stick. The stick is burning before it touches a piece and consequently does not mar the glass.

We once tried to build one of these continuous annealing lehrs. It was about five feet long, too short for an effective cooling curve, but we did get a few pieces out unbroken. One of these was annealed lying on its side and I moved it by shoving a cold thin rod in the open neck. Later it checked with an almost circular crack where the rod had touched it.

I have noticed that glass in the annealing oven at the soaking temperature is extremely fragile. The slightest touch with a sharp material will scratch it. A small bump from another piece, especially on the lip or any thin section, will fracture it. This is not a serious problem in a continuous annealing lehr in industry, but in our small periodic annealing kilns, where we wish to squeeze in "one last piece," it is a factor to consider.

One often hears of annealing in hot sand or a bucket of hot lime. Most pieces so annealed were paperweights made in the break periods in the old factories. The process must work, but it probably does so because spherical shapes can tolerate severe compressive strain and not because the annealing is very good. The floors of many periodic annealing ovens the world over are covered with sand, and it is logical to bury something in the hot sand to retard cooling. Andries Dirk Copier, the great Dutch glass designer, spoke of using hot ashes for annealing in his youth, and it seems reasonable that in the days of the wood-burning furnaces nothing would have been more natural than to shovel the ash from the fire box over the thick pieces, in some sort of bucket, to cool them more slowly. Container-annealing, simply putting something in a bucket or other closed container so that it can cool slowly, is still used in lampworking and, interestingly enough, I saw it being used to cool glass marbles made for the production of fiberglass.

Filling a container with a good granular insulator and preheating some of the material with a gather of hot glass is a way of roughly annealing simple shapes with evenly thick walls. We tried it with expanded mica or vermiculite as an insulator with some success. I have seen large beads flame-produced in Venice and cooled in a pile of reed ash on the corner of the workbench. Periodic furnaces are probably the best means of annealing, and electric resistance elements the most accurately controlled heat source for the annealing chamber.

I have seen so many ways of achieving the same results that I hesitate to tell anyone that "This is the way!" Rather, I can only say, "This is the way *I* do it." The Italians, Swedes, and Germans accomplish the same operation in different ways, and yet there may be still another way which facilitates individual styles.

It would seem that techniques which have been used to form glass for over two thousand years would be well established by now, and reduced to their simplest state. However, there has been so little teaching in the past and so little descriptive writing until now that there do not seem to be any uniform methods. Glass centers around the world seem to have discovered and rediscovered each generation's methods, tools, and equipment. The museum in Zweisel, Germany, in the midst of the Bayerwald glass region, has an old blowpipe with variations that were not understood by any of the glassworkers with whom I visited at the museum. I have included a drawing of a typical Bohemian worker's stand, completely different from the stands and benches found in most other factories. The bench is used in Germany for the man who adds the stem and foot to the stemware (see page 91). I recently saw a short film made by Andries Copier in Damascus. It showed a worker squatting on the ground in front of his furnace, rolling the pipe on his knees—certainly the first and most economical of all "benches"!

The very size and complexity of the glass factory creates a different environment. A large glass tank in a factory has very dense refractories and larger furnace ports, and the glass is worked at hotter temperatures. All of these factors combine to make it necessary to use longer pipes and shields and, in general, to make it quite uncomfortable as well as hard on your eyes. Merely to gather out of a nearly empty 250-pound glass pot in a small industrial furnace is a singeing experience.

Professional glassworkers work glass hotter in the interest of the economics of production. Working glass at a lower temperature does not require as much skill and results in a slower evolution of the form concept. Certainly, with an increase of skill, there is a tendency to work hotter in making familiar forms and to approach the speed of the factory worker.

There is a calm even in the factory as a great many men go about their tasks in the constricted space around the furnace openings. The industrial glassworker likes to preserve an air of mystery surrounding the skills he has worked so long and hard to acquire. I have seen and heard of many tricks played on would-be glassblowers visiting the factory, anticipating their first glass experience. The most common is to give the novice a cold or plugged blowpipe. The cold pipe will not pick up any glass, and the experience is quite frustrating. I was told about one boy who was given a plugged blowpipe and who blew until he fainted. The factory is certainly the worst school anyone could possibly imagine. Is it any wonder that our popular image of Hell could be taken directly from the flickering shadows and intense activity of the old glass factory?

When I was in Venice in 1958, the Martinuzzi dalla Venezia factory was still using wood for direct firing of their furnace during the working hours (oil was used at night for melting). The soot had blackened the whole interior of the furnace room so that the light level was low and the light of the furnace and the hot glass was even more dramatic. The flames and sparks leaped up as the wood was fed in periodically, and the boys gathering and carrying bits moved about in what seemed to be a demonic dance pattern overseen by the calm masters of each working group, or shop. The song "Volare," which later became so popular in the United States, would burst out every so often and be taken up by the young men all over the place. It is a picture that never dims in my memory. The vitality of Italy and the best Italian glass is exemplified by the picture; but, sadly enough, the men were making glass clowns for the tourist trade.

There is no one ideal studio setup. The amount of space itself influences the quality of the work produced. Because of the increased space in my new workshop, I find myself making bigger and, at the same time, more disciplined forms. Furthermore, the dimensions of the tools must be suited to the individual. Since each artist is of a different height and build, benches, furnace openings, yokes, and all working surfaces must be scaled to suit the individual. For example, the length of the pipes is influenced not only by the furnace heat but also by the artist's height; they must be long enough to prevent him from getting burned in the gathering, but short enough for him to blow with the piece in a somewhat vertical position, with the glass pointed downward.

The advantages of the personalized working environment cannot be measured. For a calm working atmosphere, a small furnace conveniently arranged in the working space to allow unhurried movement is a necessity. The familiarity that comes from knowing, without having to think deliberately about the location of each tool, the height of the bench, or any other parts of the glassblowing process, is a great aid to any artist.

Successful work in glass depends on the integration of the body's movements with the fluidity of the molten glass. Each new procedure must flow from its predecessor. Additional tools are incorporated unhesitatingly into the artist's dance without interrupting the growth of form. It is in this flow that new needs arise and are satisfied by the grasping of an old tool in a new way, or by using a different motion in response to the situation. It is in this way that the evolution of new skills and new forms occurs. In the response of the man, his hands, and his body musculature to the heat of the furnace and the glass—as the eye follows the moving delineations of the flowing ball in front of him, as it grows, elongates, and swells—precise learned skill and exact tools are unimportant. Even a pad of wet newspaper, folded into a flat square large enough to cover the hand and wrist, will serve to manipulate the form and to coax out the shape.

Technique must never be an end in itself. The value derived from the incorporation of old or the development of new techniques is not in itself art. It is merely an external vehicle for the internal expression or statement by the artist. The extent of variation, innovation, or limitation in technique is always determined by the scope of the artist's ability to manipulate both himself and his material at any given moment. He must be able to improvise.

Improvisation is a much more valid approach to technique than the traditional methods of the skilled craftsman. As I understand from Sybren Valkema, Dutch designer and teacher of design, many of the techniques now used in the production at Leerdam in the Netherlands came about because the workers and designers did not know the traditional methods and were forced to devise their own. The characteristic swelling of the form above the thick base in many pieces occurred naturally as the men were working with large gathers on the punty and inflating them with compressed air rather than blowing in the normal manner. It was by improvisation, too, that the glass artist broke the dominance of the "master craftsman" and produced work of exceptional quality for the system within which he was employed.

When Erwin Eisch, the highly skilled and highly imaginative Bavarian glass artist, and his assistant Karl Paternoster visited me in 1967, they did several large bowls in my studio. With a magic motorized camera we were able to capture the movements of many of the techniques. Most of the action took place at an approximation of the Bavarian-Bohemian working table. There was a water tank holding the blocks, paddles, etc., about waist high, and fastened to it was a yoke. The blocking and tooling were accomplished standing, rotating the pipe left-handed in the yoke, rather than on the two arm supports of the bench. In Erwin's factory in Frauenau, the bench is used mainly for making the feet.

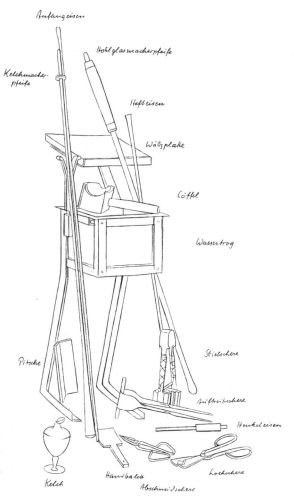

BOHEMIAN WORKER'S STAND:
THE EUROPEAN GLASSWORKER WORKS STANDING UP.
(DRAWING REPRODUCED FROM *REISE ZU DEN GLASBLÄSERN,* PUBLISHED BY VEREINIGTEN LAUSITZER GLASWERKE AKTIENGESELLSCHAFT, ZWICKAU, 1938.)

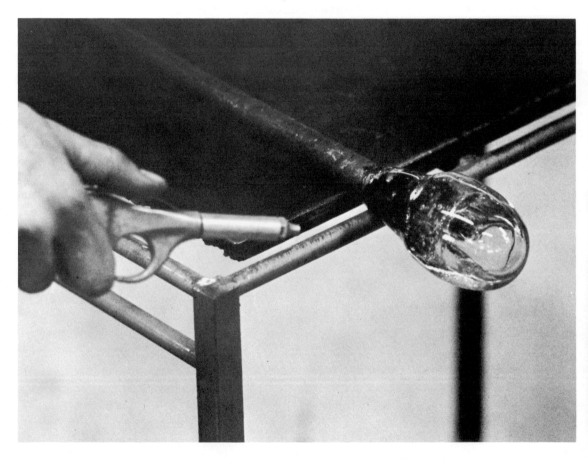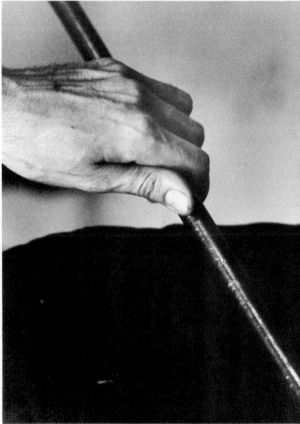

The initial bubble was blown out with little marvering so that the end was thin. Rather than marver, they usually use the bottom of the block, which has been cut into a shallow trough. We made a curved tool in approximately the same shape to hold in the hand. He cooled the bubble a little with an air hose because the glass was very long-working. This allowed him to make his second gather quickly. The rotation of the pipe at the yoke was a beautiful rhythmic movement. The pipe rolled over the palm of the hand and was kept in motion by the fingers moving in sequence.

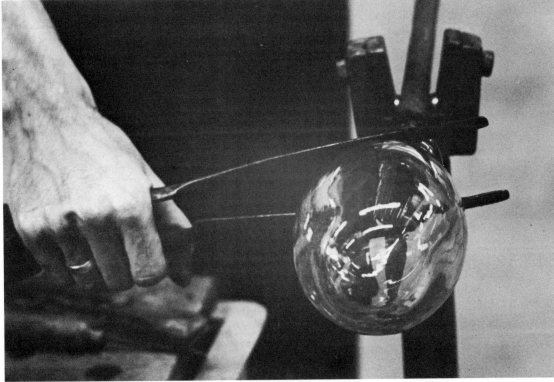

Succeeding gathers were blocked and expanded. Erwin was able to control the hotter glass by chilling the forward part of the sphere so that he could neck in the glass part next to the blowpipe with the jacks. Later this allowed the piece to be broken off the pipe more easily.

Using a bit gathered by Karl, Erwin pulled down on it to start a cane and cut it off so that a thread of colored glass could be wound on the form. Several blobs of colored glass were also added after warming the whole piece in the glory hole. Erwin used a hook to draw the thread into festoons on the surface. Another gather was then added over the piece and blocked and marvered. The bottom was flattened with a large wet wooden paddle, the steam driving a small concave indentation in the bottom which was reshaped with a pad of wet newspaper. Then, at the bench, a punty was stuck on the center of the base with a square shears used to guide the attachment. After scratching the indentation made earlier with a wet file, the blowpipe was tapped and the neck broken away.

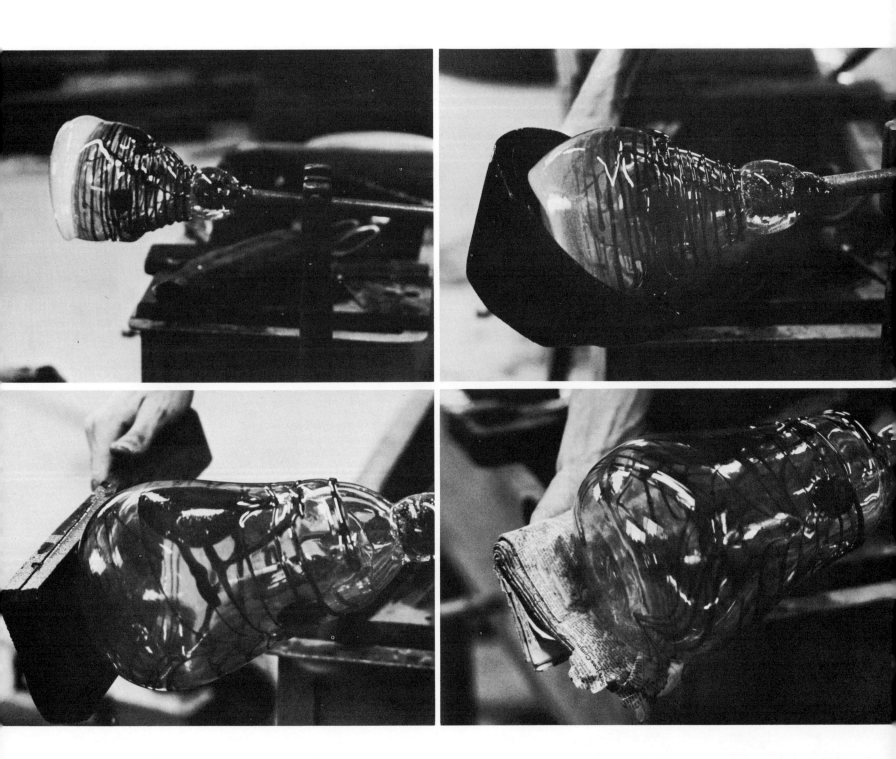

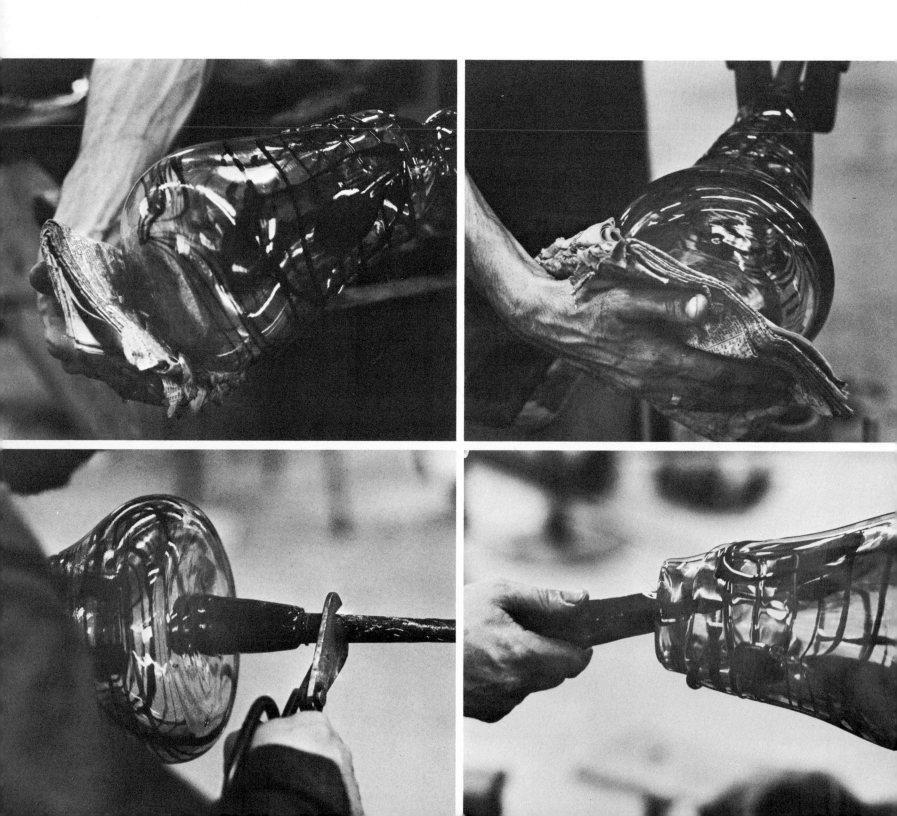

The neck was carefully opened out with a wet stick, reheated, and cut with straight shears. Generally, Erwin cut around more than once to make the cut straight. The shears pushed against the cut edge and straightened themselves out so that the cut was perpendicular to the axis of the form.

Erwin did not spin out the form but used paddles inside and out to develop the bowl shape. The piece was fumed heavily in the process of opening it, with the result that there were characteristic tiny vertical lines in the crinkled surface from the stretching after fuming and reheating. The bowl was opened further, again with wooden paddles. The finished bowl was characteristic of several done in the different glasses.

Another sequence that was extremely interesting was the use of a mold by Erwin and Karl to produce a footed candlestick. They began with a double gather of a dark glass. Mold-blown ware is made from a much softer glass than that used to make the same kind of form without the mold; softer glass gives a more faithful reproduction of the form of the mold. The glass almost seemed to flow down into the mold by itself. Steam holes drilled into the broadest points of the mold prevent the formation of steam pressure pockets which hinder the duplication of the shape of the mold.

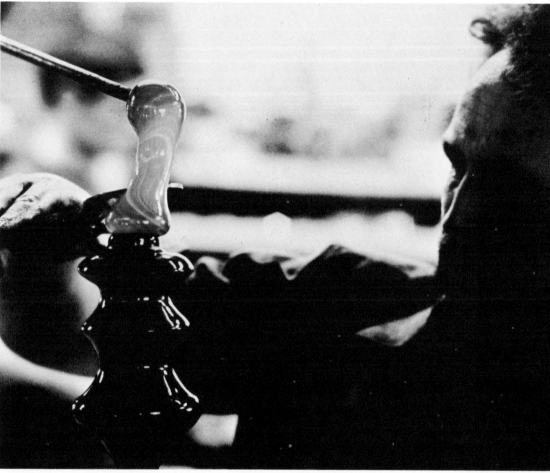

Once out of the mold, the form was straightened in preparation for a new gather to be draped onto the vertical form. After being cut by the square shears, the gather for the foot was patted flat, and the piece was lowered to the bench for shaping with the footing tool. This tool is cut to the size of the base of the mold. The footing tool was raised until it was in contact with the solid base of the foot, and was slowly pressed onto the soft gob of the foot, flattening and spreading it. The thickness of the foot was controlled by the small brass stop in the footing tool.

When the shaping was completed, the punty was quickly attached; in a footed piece the thin foot becomes chilled and reheating it is difficult without causing distortion. The neck was cracked off and reheated. Prior to opening, the piece was straightened on the punty with a wooden paddle. It was then opened with a jack and trimmed. Trimming the neck should always be done from the bottom of the piece. If the piece is cut from the top, the shearing re-attaches itself.

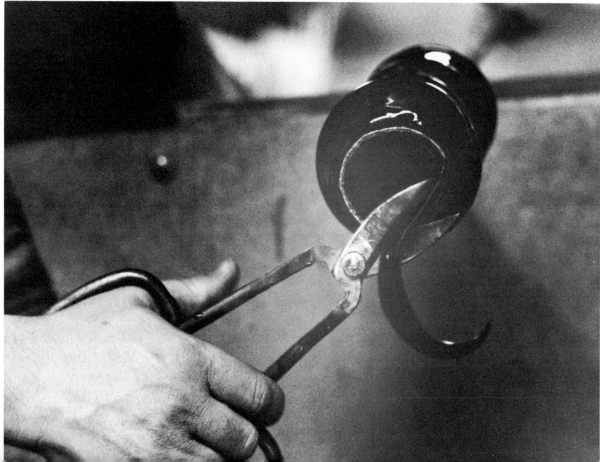

Once trimmed, the neck was opened and flared with the jacks and the piece knocked off.

7 A Note on Safety

All glass-forming materials are dangerous. We work at very high temperatures, and no matter how familiar we are with furnaces and hot materials, they are always dangerous. Normally innocuous materials at high temperatures are often more potent than the most powerful acids. Dangerous fumes are always given off by the melting glass. Finally, hot glass burns and cold broken glass cuts very easily.

We are all familiar with the sharp spears of broken sheet glass, and we handle them gingerly. But cold glass lumps of unannealed cullet can have great stresses within them that can cause them to explode, sending fragments outward with great force. Furthermore, excess water dripping from blocks and other wet tools on lumps of hot cullet can cause them to explode. Cullet should be kept in proper containers not only for housekeeping reasons, but also so that if there are delayed explosions they will take place inside a good steel box or drum rather than in the open where they cause harm to both men and equipment. In working it is difficult to tell which is cool and which is hot cullet, and so all cullet containers should be made of metal. The cullet pan by the bench for shearings is quite important. Visitors to the studio are often first attracted to the bright bit of cullet in the pan, and if not cautioned, they are easily burned or cut, as the glass retains enough heat to cause a bad burn for some time after it looks cool.

Burns occur with some frequency in the beginning, but as the student becomes more familiar with the tools and processes, they occur less frequently. We have found that ice applied immediately to burns will relieve both the pain and the severity of the injury. In working with glass, burns often occur because tools are out of place or in an awkward position. Perhaps the biggest danger is with the artist himself. Haste, fatigue, or exceeding the limits of one's ability to control the glass are all very common causes of trouble.

The extreme glare of the hot furnace, especially at the temperatures necessary to melt the harder glasses, is dangerous to the eyes. A shield or window for looking directly into the furnace does help. Some students have purchased the didymium glasses used by flameworkers; these effectively filter out the dangerous yellow sodium glare.

In mixing batch, the best thing to do is to consider all of the chemicals to be poisonous, since in one way or another they are. The worst chemicals, like arsenic, can be absorbed through the skin just from handling. Some, such as lead, zinc, and barium compounds, accumulate in the body and result in heavy metal poisoning. Silica, although not toxic in these ways, gave its name to the respiratory disease silicosis, caused by the inhalation of inorganic, insoluble dusts. Other water-soluble chemicals, especially the strong alkalis, cause burns in the throat and lungs if their dust is inhaled. Cleanliness, rubber gloves, dust inhalators, chemical masks, and reasonable care are essential to safety in mixing batch.

In melting, a good hood to draw off the gases is a necessary part of any furnace.

When using natural gas it is wise to have on hand some safety devices for emergencies. A solenoid shut-off valve to cut off gas in case of a power failure is standard in installations using a forced draft burner. Some inspectors, however, will demand a great deal more: a constant pilot, a mixing valve, and a flame sensor tied to shut-off valves in both the electrical and the gas lines. In some cases where there are extreme variations in gas pressure, a pressure regulator in addition to the gas valve regulating the burner may be required.

Installation of gas heat in a glass furnace is different from normal installation for gas heat because in a glass furnace there is positive ignition from the incandescent furnace and the burner is on continuously for months at a time. Normally, trouble occurs when a motor fails in the forced air fan. The gas keeps on burning with a smoky yellow flame, and in a small furnace the heat drops down slowly to below red heat in a period of five or six hours. If the gas supply is interrupted for a short time, which is more unusual, and the air supply continues to blow on the glass, there is danger of a gas build-up and an explosion if the air has cooled the glass to below red heat.

Considering possible mishaps, unless you have had a great deal of experience using gas heat it is best to seek professional advice and to follow code recommendations.

8 Form & Glassblowing

Form comes not from inspiration; it is born of work. Artists do not imagine forms and then execute them. It is naive to suppose that in art forms are transferred, as if they were templates, from mind to matter. This is the distinction between the work of the artist and the production of artisans, designers, and businessmen in collaboration. This collaboration has established weights and counterweights which prevent the influence of chance. The ultimate accomplishment in industry is the perfect realization of a scheme; it is a compromise.

Improvisation is a response to a given moment of involvement with the material which in the heat of work is followed to a logical conclusion or exploited to open up a new direction. Many times we hear people dismiss such creations as accidents. I prefer to characterize them in another way, as the "action-reaction-action-reaction" sequence of the growing dialogue between artist and material.

I once asked the late Carlos Lopez, painter and professor of art at the University of Michigan, how he knew when a particular painting was finished. He answered, "It isn't easy, but I always know when I've gone too far." I am sure that every artist faces this problem. Every piece goes through a thousand or more potential shapes. When watching another glassworker produce a piece, I often feel the urge to shout, "Stop!"

In Erwin Eisch's factory in Germany I found myself in the position of "master," not because of any great skill, but because I could adapt to the problems of a new form more quickly than the skilled worker. My attention was focused on the piece in hand and I would do whatever was necessary at any given moment to realize its potential as I saw it. This is not generally comparable to the attitude of the factory worker. Because his techniques are adapted to a given product, and his equipment developed for that end, he is seldom equipped to help in solving a problem. He is not focused on deviation or improvisation, but rather on the achievement of a pre-established goal.

The study of someone involved in blowing glass can set off a whole reverberation of form in one's own work, because each person sees some different potential in the series, his own termination to the forming process. There seems to be an urge to get into it with a paddle, or to have it blown a little more. To watch such a process becomes a challenge.

Working with a powerful personality can create an almost overwhelming problem. During the time Erwin Eisch was working in my studio, and for some weeks after he left, his influence was so strong that I found myself working a series of forms so derivative that my wife complained she did not know my forms from Erwin's. I had to reorganize the studio, putting out of sight the direct influence of those pieces, and begin to work with a very restricted form concept, working out of it into a new form vehicle. I found the same influence true again when working in Erwin's studio in Germany. I had to restrict myself to working with forms I had been doing in America. Moving up into the open factory, there to work with the factory glass, I was able to break out in new directions. I am sure the student faces this problem, especially where there is only one instructor in a medium. For this reason I have always had my studio separate from that of my students.

Within a year I had two occasions to work with Erwin Eisch. First, Erwin was in Wisconsin as a visiting artist at the University in November and December of 1967. The following summer I was his guest in Bavaria for about a month. He produced about two hundred pieces in my workshop for exhibition here

JUG BY ERWIN EISCH, 1966,
SHOWING PERFECT INTEGRATION
OF PAINTING AND FORM.

in America, and I produced thirty sculptural pieces at his factory in Frauenau for exhibition in Europe. The experience was rewarding and informative, especially in view of the necessity of finding solutions to technical problems that were beyond our abilities to foresee.

My experience during these two periods are recounted below, in diary form, for the insight they may provide the student into the techniques, the problems, the improvisations, and the excitement which are part of our work with glass.

Verona, Wisconsin

Wednesday, November 15

From the moment I picked up Erwin Eisch and his assistant, Karl Paternoster, at O'Hare Airport in Chicago, we began to work out the schedule for the month he was to work with me. On arriving at the farm we went directly to my studio to see the new furnaces and other equipment I had built in preparation for the work. I had a single furnace filled with 475 marbles so that Erwin might begin working immediately to get the feel of both the equipment and the studio.

Thursday, November 16

Erwin and Karl worked with the 475 marbles while George, my assistant, and I set up the batch-mixing area. For the actual mixing we used an old tub from a grinding machine and a garden hoe. A wooden box with slanted ends made of ¾'' plywood would work as well. Erwin said that at home he mixed in a wheelbarrow. (Dominick Labino has worked out a simple ball-mill, which seems excellent, using croquet balls and a 30-gallon steel drum mounted on a shaft penetrating the drum at an angle so as to cause it to rotate in an eccentric manner.) We did not have dust masks so we used damp towels over our faces. Since many of the materials are caustic or poisonous, a good mask is imperative.

We had planned to start melting a batch of glass from one of the two formulas Erwin had sent me. On checking the temperature of my larger furnace with an optical pyrometer he had brought with him, Erwin was not sure we could melt even the softer of the two formulas (see table of formulas at end of chapter). Although I had started the furnace as soon as we had returned from the airport, it was still not hot enough. Before melting a glass, the furnace must be very hot, since the batch as it is placed inside chills the furnace. Quick melting is necessary in order to benefit from the stirring action of the gases as they pass off.

Since I had not been able to obtain potassium nitrate, we made several small changes in the softer formula, adding additional potash for the potassium nitrate and cutting down on the cryolite, as eight units in the original formula seemed too high. I also felt that since we were using powdered flint instead of glassmaker's sand, we would not need quite as much heat to get the silica in solution.

Friday, November 17

We continued to work with the 475, but charged the furnace containing the batch formula. Erwin found the 475 too stiff to work and too hard to anneal by his standards.

Saturday, November 18

Testing the batch glass on Saturday morning, we found it to be a beautiful amber. I had to be away most of the day, leaving Erwin to work on his own. When I returned I found we were annealing at too high a temperature for the new glass. The 475 had required a temperature of 1035°F., while this

glass began to sag at 875°F. Consequently, some of the pieces were sagged. There was no reason we could find for the amber color (although it was beautiful), since we had added no coloring oxide. As soon as we could get potassium nitrate, which would act as an oxidizer in the melting, we intended to go back to the original formula, suspecting both carbon from reduction and sulfur from the sodium sulfate had produced the yellow color. In the meantime, since the glass was already amber, the addition of silver in nitrate form could not hurt it. We added the silver to one of the smaller furnaces and manganese carbonate to another, giving us three colors to work with on Monday. We did substitute more soda ash for the sodium sulfate to dilute the amber tint in the clear tank.

Monday, November 20

Monday morning found we had been quite successful; the three colors were beautiful. The clear glass, however, was bubbly. We never did get enough heat to clear the glass perfectly in an overnight cycle until we had made more drastic changes in the formula. The glass would clear—or fine, as glassmakers call it—in two days, but not overnight as we had wished.

Tuesday, November 21

We cleaned the clear tank and melted the softer formula with the addition of the potassium nitrate.

Wednesday, November 22

Erwin had a habit of not cleaning his pipes, but resting them back on the edge of the tank after finishing a piece in order to keep them hot. He had left his pipes from the batch containing the manganese carbonate on the tank containing the newly melted clear batch. This contaminated the clear glass with a slight purple tint. Because the glass was still workable, we used it that day. But we cleaned it out at the evening break and melted a new batch for Friday. (Thursday was Thanksgiving and we also wanted to see if another day of melting would clear the glass of seeds.)

Friday, November 24

In melting 475 cullet previously, I had found that I could clear the glass by cooling it. This either squeezed the gases into solution or dissolved them into the liquid in the same way that the carbonation in soft drinks is dissolved under pressure in the sealed bottle. The cooling glass shrinks, creating sufficient pressure to accomplish this in 475 glass at a temperature above red heat. I did not cool the longer-working, more fluid glass we were melting long enough to accomplish this. Needless to say, we still had seeds on Friday. We then tried the addition of arsenic—one pound to about one hundred pounds of glass—but there was no obvious difference. About this time I began work on the burners to improve our heat. We continued to work with the tank of manganese glass and added some cobalt in the form of powder blue to another tank in which I had melted some silver cullet.

Tuesday, November 28

We again tried the formula of the main batch of clear glass, adding more cryolite, cutting back the borax, and leaving out the arsenic. It did not clear, but our pressure was down because we were running out of propane. We did not get a good melt, and Erwin stressed the importance of getting a good, hot initial melt to get the glass all fluid. When the furnace is charged it must be very hot and the powders are mounded up to fill the tank. As they melt they shrink down to almost half the space, so that a full tank must be charged at least twice. Erwin stressed that the first charge should be all melted and the furnace hot again before the second charge. When the tank is full there are two easy ways of telling if the glass is well melted: the first is to draw a thread and, when it is cool, to pull it through your fingers. The tiny undissolved bits of silica and other substances will cause a roughness in the glass. The other way is to blow a very thin bubble and inspect it. All the ordinary defects, such as cords, stones, and seeds, are exaggerated in this form, while opaque glass becomes practically transparent in this thin section. It is easy to understand the importance of early fluidity, when the majority of the gases are escaping, to create a strong stirring action which gives a homogeneous solution and sweeps the liquid clear.

Wednesday, November 29

They added four ounces of copper per thirty pounds of batch to the tank containing the silver glass, and one ounce of powder blue per thirty pounds of batch to the furnace containing manganese. The colors were strong and vivid.

Erwin did not want transparency or translucence, as he was working with small, involved sculptural forms, and the confusion of the transmitted light and inner lines and surfaces broke up his forms. Consequently, the strong colors were just to his liking. To combat the highly reflective surface he resorted to fuming and later to enameling. (Fuming is the coating of the surface with a thin spray of metallic chlorides such as tin and iron; this leaves a very thin coating about one-quarter of a wave length of light thick on the surface. This refracts the light, breaking it into its component colors as the light passes through the film to the surface of the glass; is reflected back through the film to the surface of the glass; and back through the film again. The fumed surface shrinks, giving a wrinkled surface which diffuses the light. This is, of course, the surface quality of the Tiffany and other Art Nouveau iridescent glass.) We simply put the chlorides in a shallow pan under the hood of the furnace and created a thick smoke by putting small gathers of hot glass in the pan. Each piece was then rotated in the smoke and warmed in the glory hole.

We fumed most of Erwin's pieces. Earlier, in working with the silver and manganese glass, we had found the fuming to be especially beautiful, transforming the denser concentration of silver into the most brilliant rainbow colors.

Left:
FIGURE MADE AND DECORATED BY EISCH
IN THE AUTHOR'S STUDIO, 1967.

Right:
OPAQUE FUMED FIGURE BY EISCH.

Thursday, November 30

Erwin decided he wanted an opal glass. Since we were using cryolite anyway, we decided to increase it to eight units, as in the original formula, to get a fluorine opal. We also added zinc oxide to counteract the extreme fluidity of the cryolite. Unknown to me, Erwin decided eight units was not enough cryolite and increased it to sixteen! When we tested the glass after the first charge had melted down, the glass came out white and solid as soon as it cooled in the air. As a consequence, we charged the second time with greatly reduced amounts of cryolite, trying to even out the formula.

Friday, December 1

The glass was not thick and was almost clear of seeds. It struck opal readily, and they were able to work with it. The slow annealing made it strike even better, although I found it hard to work because it set up very fast.

Wednesday, December 5

We had run out of materials, and since we would have differing sources for our chemicals, and their compositions would not duplicate exactly those we had used till now, I decided to round off the numbers on the formula, making it easier to work with. I could mix two hundred pounds at once, so I started with a hundred-pound bag of flint and fifty pounds of soda ash so that they made up 50 percent and 25 percent of the batch. This glass worked out quite well. In our first glass I had tried a little sodium sulfate, but it did not help in the melting. I also increased the amount of zinc and changed the source of calcium to dolomite, the dolomite introducing magnesium as part of the calcium requirement. This made the glass noticeably easier to fine. We decided to stay with this glass since it fined overnight quite well, was easy to work, and was quite brilliant, the high barium content affecting its index of refraction.

My notes indicate that in the furnace where we had the best flame, the glass was very good. We then took apart and cleaned the other burners and produced better glass as a result. Erwin at this point began to work to finish his pieces for exhibition, making fewer each day, while I began to work with the glass more and more. We tried a few other colors, neodymium, chromium, and finally some iron. The neodymium was proportioned one pound to thirty pounds of batch for a beautiful light gray-blue which changed to a violet in incandescent light. The chrome green was predictable, but the iron over a period of days became better and better. It changed from a heavy dark green to a fine blue-green of quite a different character from the others. The slight reduction in the aspiration natural draft burner was certainly influential in producing a better green.

Once Erwin left on December 15, I continued to melt glass, changing the formula a few times more as listed in the table at the end of the chapter. Each change made an appreciable difference in the quality and workability of the glass.

"GLÜCK UND GLAS,"
VASE BY ERWIN EISCH, 1967.
THE PIECE WAS A HOUSE GIFT TO THE AUTHOR.

I went to Frauenau the next spring to work in Erwin's factory in preparation for an exhibit of my work. The Eisch factory is a family affair that has grown from a glass-cutting workshop in the home to a factory employing 250 workers. When, around 1951, the larger German glass factories cut off the supply of blanks—vases, stemware, and other forms—to the independent glass cutters, the craftsmen were forced either to work for the large factories or to begin their own production. The fiercely independent Eisches set up their own furnace in the building that is now Erwin's home and painting studio. Erwin, the eldest of the three brothers, serves as designer for the factory; the next brother is director, and the youngest, master cutter. Their mother and father still work as craftsmen in the factory, as do numerous aunts, uncles, cousins, and in-laws.

Frauenau, Germany

Wednesday, June 12

Erwin looked at his glass through a safety mask, a small piece of cobalt window glass in a square wooden form with a tiny mouth holder projecting from the bottom to grab in your teeth, so as to leave your hands free. Not being satisfied with the glass, he took a small, wet stick impaled on the pointed end of a ten-foot rod and shoved it to the bottom of the batch. Huge bubbles the size of the pot rose and broke; Erwin's glass was bad. The manganese batch had some lumps of hard glass but was not stony, the clear had large stones. The furnace was not hot enough.

I remembered that that morning he had taken his burner tip out to the machine shop for cleaning. I had thought the night before that his furnace was no hotter than mine, and that the batch which had just been charged was not bubbling. He charged again now, and the furnace seemed a little cold, but the burner looked clean and he seemed satisfied. As it turned out, the glass was still not very good and took another day to improve.

Thursday, June 13

The pots were recharged at 8 P.M. At midnight Erwin turned down the furnaces after first frothing the glass with wood impaled on the ¾" rod. Yesterday's glass was out of the annealing oven and was full of stones and lumps in between the stones and cords.

Together, Erwin and I blew spheres and cylinders meant for cutting. The glass in the manganese pot worked beautifully. As the furnace was a little cold, he turned it up, and we emptied it, but it was not clean enough as it turned out. We felt it was melting right at that moment. The pot nearest the flame was the colder of the two, so that one (the manganese color) needed cullet, since cullet lowers the temperature necessary to melt batch. We came in at 9 P.M. to bubble the glass with wood. With a word to the night schmeltzer to turn it down at midnight, we went to bed.

Friday, June 14

Erwin said he would put a little more potash in the batch. This meant an increase from two to six kilos of potash to make the glass soften and to get rid of the cords and stones.

I had to do some cutting and found out that the bad glass was very difficult to work. All of the forms that were doubled over were badly annealed, and the thick and thin spheres could not be cut; even the thin tubes could not be cut. The cordiness and lumps were very bright in the scope.

Monday, June 17

Karl worked with me in Erwin's studio. The glass was better and the top of the clear glass (which they call weiss, or white glass) was almost perfect, although it got worse as we worked it down. The glass from the factory suited me better since it had more refraction and not too heavy a color: a light chrome and a warm brown amber. The small furnace in Erwin's studio had a potash-manganese and the color was also rather brown in the contaminated clear pot.

The factory is slowly changing and prospering under Erwin's influence. They tried some sample pieces of white opal cased with potash-manganese and a brown, probably selenium. These samples were made from Erwin's glass from his furnace, and were made compatible, but when there were orders to fill, there was a problem in producing the glasses in the factory furnace. The glasses matched as to their coefficient of expansion, but they were so different in their annealing temperatures, or curves, that they cracked at the very end of the lehr. The factory could not melt Erwin's glass because it was too soft for the other ten pots heated jointly in the big furnace. So they had to make the opal quite hard, which they chose to do with lime. Their first change was to add more barium, but the lady at the end of the lehr said, as the first test pieces came through, "Kaput!" Some small sample melts from a little pot furnace would have been a big help here, but I do not think they trusted anything but an actual pot melt in the regular furnace and a shop working in the regular way. When I returned a few weeks later, the problem was solved and they were in production.

Batch Formulas

	Labino's Formula	Eisch's Original Formula	Nov.17	Nov.21	Nov.28	Opal Nov.30	Dec.5	Dec.16	Dec.27	Jan.3	Apr.10	Eisch's June 11
Flint	45.5	48	48	48	48	48	50	50	50	50	50	75
Soda Ash	10	24	25.5	25.5	24	24	25	25	25	25	25	35
Borax	10.5	1	2	2	1	1	2	2	2	2	2	2
Dolomite	7.5						5	5	2.5	2.5	4	
Fluorospar	1.25											
Barium Carbonate		5.5	5.5	5.5	5.5	5.5	5	5	5	5	5	7
Whiting		3.5	3.5	3.5	3.5	3.5			2.5	2.5	2	7
Zinc Oxide						1	2	2	2	3	2	
Potash		5	7	5	5	5	5	5	5	5	5	3
Potassium Nitrate		1.6		1.6	1.6	1.6	2	2	3	3	3	1
Cryolite		8	2.5	2.5	4	10	5	5	3	3	4	
Sodium Sulfate		2					1					2
Arsenic				.5					.25			
Antimony									.25			
Nepheline Syenite	5									(a pinch)		
Cobalt										(a pinch)		
Selenium										(a pinch)		

9 Present & Future

There are many directions stemming from equipment and techniques not discussed in this book, such as cutting, assemblage, engraving, electroforming, etching, sawing, lost-wax casting, sagging, laminating, enameling, sand-blasting, and carving. My students have tried, with a variety of success, all of these techniques, as they were first challenged by the forms of the past. I do not think everyone must enjoy every phase of glassworking or respond to all of the directions we see exemplified in past work. It is interesting to see the speed with which many students pass beyond the traditional concepts of glassblowing. A few have rejected the traditional approach from the start. On seeing the glass for the first time, one of my students was prompted to bring a waffle iron to class. From it he produced a pressed piece, which, when mounted in a box with three mirrored sides and a mirrored bottom, gave a brilliance none of us thought possible with our 475 glass.

Unfortunately, some of the most experimental work has yet to be seen. In fact, some exhibitions have rejected these pieces because they did not conform to the "expressive qualities" of our earlier work. When a jury or the critics decide that maturity has already been reached and the experimental stage is over, they essentially deny new concepts. Sometime ago I was criticized because I had forsaken the exciting and expressive "fluidity" of my first pieces. Glass and art have so many faces that critics should be prepared to see many conflicting directions. This is not to deny what has been done, but to say that anything can inspire an artist to branch off in new directions: a new tool, perhaps, or an old form seen in a different context. Artists question their own directions continually.

Can a direction run out of steam? Have legitimate directions in art lost their legitimacy, or only their pertinence to a particular moment? Is work legitimate just because it is the best a given artist can produce? Are we concerned with a movement or style?

I maintain that great things are possible and are happening in glass, and will continue to happen if the conditions set forth in this book are maintained. The future was in doubt in 1959, and it continued to be in doubt until the mid-1960s, when experiments in glassworking became the expressions of the artists' own directions. Artist-produced glass is not in itself a style.

We have been very concerned with seeing glass. One of my students has suggested that another world awaits us when we learn what there is to see *through* glass. The magical world of optics and light transmitted through and trapped by our forms is yet to be approached. With the diamond saw we are looking into glass, into the interior of the form. We have been constructing glass boxes for years to look out of—to see the passing world from our picture windows. The room of mirrors, an environmental sculpture shown at The Art Institute of Chicago, is a suggestion for tomorrow. The ethereal quality of the window, the wall that we barely see, huge planes so commonplace they should hold nothing for us, can be bent in our ovens, can be painted with glass enamels, can be fastened together to change our view, to create illusion, to make a new vision. Lines can hang in space, planes can protrude, colors can recede and disappear.

In America, the emphasis has always been on the individual, whether in teaching or personal development. This concept is inextricably bound to the development of the artist. The concept of the artist-glassblower, though relatively recent, recognizes the necessity of each artist's exploration in his own direction in his search for form. Each personal exploration is unique in its experiences, but all such

Opposite—
Top left:
THIS VASE BY AN UNKNOWN CZECH ARTIST IS STRUCK BOTH YELLOW AND RED.

Top center:
"ARIEL," SWEDISH GLASS MADE AT ORREFORS IN THE 1950s. (COURTESY OF THE CORNING MUSEUM OF GLASS.)

Top right:
BOTTLES BY PAOLO VENINI, MADE IN THE 1950s. (COURTESY OF THE CORNING MUSEUM OF GLASS.)

Bottom left:
GLASS SCULPTURE FOR THE CZECHOSLOVAKIAN PAVILION AT EXPO 67 IN MONTREAL, BY RENE RUBICEK.

Bottom right:
WINDOW MURAL BY STANISLAV AND JAROSLAVA LIBENSKY.

Above:
THE INTERIOR OF A GERMAN GLASS FACTORY.
(DRAWING REPRODUCED FROM *REISE ZU DEN
GLASBLÄSERN*, PUBLISHED BY VEREINIGTEN
LAUSITZER GLASWERKE AKTIENGESELLSCHAFT,
ZWICKAU, 1938.)

Right:
VASE BY DOMINICK LABINO.
(COLLECTION OF THE ARTIST.)

searches are characterized by the doubts, decisions, successes, and failures involved in the struggle for direction. In my own case, I cannot support my work in glass on two levels; I cannot create some things for the commercial market and others for experimentation.

I could feel satisfied making functional individual pottery in 1956, but I cannot justify its production today. I feel pressures of time and the attack on my values far more intensely today, and I feel I must respond in a more definitive manner.

This is a different time from the fifties, when the small artist-potteries were flourishing under the Leach philosophy of providing artist-produced wares for household use. A man cannot so dissipate himself today in the face of an industry geared to mass production and consumption. He must distill his essence and demand recognition for his real contribution. It is only in this way that individual values will be conserved in the face of a computerized society. Mass production in an industry of the 1950s, where production was controlled by men, is totally different from the 1960s or 1970s, where these same machines are controlled by computers. The attack on the individual values exemplified in creative work grows stronger in our computerized society. The force to combat it, to balance it, must not be diluted.

For me the turning point, the change from the still functional container forms to ''broken open'' forms, came in 1963. These smashed, remelted, ''double bubble'' shapes were my first obvious denial of function. All I did from that time on was a function of my attempts to get at the essence of the material. The potential of my first irrational act of fusing and finishing a form that I had smashed in an act of displeasure was not immediately recognizable to me. The piece lay in the studio for some weeks before I ground the bottom and brought it in the house. It aroused such immediate antipathy in my wife that I looked at it much more closely, finally deciding to send it to an exhibition. Its refusal there made me even more obstinate, and I took it to New York to show with the other more established forms included in my exhibition at the Museum of Contemporary Crafts in January 1964. Although it was not displayed then, I later showed it to the curators of design at the Museum of Modern Art. They, perhaps relating it to some other neo-Dada work in the museum, purchased it for the Design Collection.

When my ego returned to normal, diminishing the sense of triumph over the opinions of my wife and the jury which had rejected the piece, I found myself working more and more in an abstract manner, using container forms only as exercises to perfect my skill in blowing. But the initial breakthrough, structured through an experience which has been labeled by some art critics as a ''happy accident,'' freed me from the container shape and led me into a whole new area of broken-open forms. These forms progressed from the collapsed form, the juxtaposition of collapsed forms, and now the cutting open of forms. With a new sense of discipline, I also made a series of very simple spheres and faceted vases.

In a recent publication of the Notsjo Glassworks, a subsidiary of the Arabia Ceramic Factory in Finland, there was a reference to a cylinder blown for window glass on a huge blowpipe weighing twenty pounds, the glass to be split later and heated so that it would lie flat (a process still being used at the Blenko Works in Milton, West Virginia). The cylinder was fourteen feet high and sixteen inches in diameter!

Work on this scale is not beyond the artist's capabilities in an assemblage. I do not believe that there is any particular virtue in size for its own sake; but there are some artists who feel that unless the material can be executed on a large scale, it has no value to them.

Under the leadership of Andries Copier, the great designer, now-retired, at the Leerdam factory in the Netherlands, there was, in the summer of 1966, an outdoor exhibition entitled ''The Interplay of Glass and Light.'' Huge forms were constructed in a park, the garden of Weverij de Ploeg, Bergyk. Although there were some specially made blown pieces, commercially available glass was used for the most part. The photographs are most dramatic, but the assemblages were taken apart since the show was meant only to dramatize and publicize the availability of the materials. Nevertheless the sculptural possibilities for the artist in glass were very apparent.

In Europe, the glass artists are very excited by the prospect of working on their own. Recently there have been some amazing things produced.

The work of Stanislav and Jaroslava Libensky of Czechoslovakia is the most exciting I have seen. The scale and the scope of their work as seen at Expo 67 in Montreal, were startling and point the way to the scale of the future.

The Libensky conceptions were cast in fairly conventional forms: window murals, free-standing

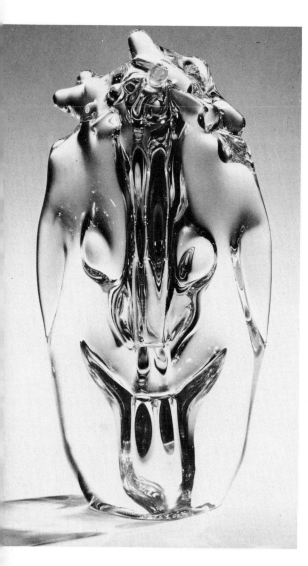

MASK BY SYBREN VALKEMA.

Opposite:
SCULPTURAL WORK BY WILLEM HEESEN.
(COURTESY OF N. V. KONINKLIJKE NEDERLANDSCHE GLASFABRIEK "LEERDAM.")

panels, and a huge cone, all made by means of lost-wax castings. They used precast, factory-produced blocks provided by the government, which were sagged into investment molds in large electric furnaces. The scale was such that up to three weeks were required to anneal each block. There was a great deal of technical assistance, as one might expect in a socialist country where this kind of commitment was made for an international exposition. But the work was conceived in their own modeling studio in the basement of their home in Zelesny Brod. One did not sense any pressure or interference. The workshop for casting was just a few steps away and was entirely under their control.

Also contributing to the success of the Czechoslovakian exhibit at Expo was the work of René Roubicek. The glass fountain of Roubicek, architectural in form and concept, consisted of sparkling crystal glass forms strung on stainless steel upright rods in a reflecting pool that was partly within and partly outside the pavilion. The icicle-like forms created a small forest in a corner of the exhibition space and projected through the large window overlooking a wide area of the fair. The material was less interesting than the Libenskys' since it was of standard Bohemian crystal; but the scale and refractive qualities of the individual pulled and pinched forms assembled on their shining rods were quite beautiful.

Next door to the Czechoslovakian Pavilion was the Italian Pavilion, showing another direction in glass in the work of the Venetian painter Emilio Vedova. The Vedova conception was a moving light "mural" in a colossal T-shaped hall, 175 feet by 65 feet, with images projected through a series of 125 plates of colored glass made by Vedova at the Venninni factory at Murano. There were color juxtapositions and inclusions of tremendous range heightened by enlargement and projection.

Vedova's work, once the work with the hot glass was finished, was mainly with light and projected images on the wall enclosure. He, too, was able to have extensive professional technical help. He was given the use of a deconsecrated church in Venice as a studio. This huge, dramatic space must have influenced the final conception.

I had seen the work of the Libenskys and Vedova in progress, and was fortunate to be at the opening day of the fair to see their finished conceptions. The decisions of the two governments to invest in these men must be one of the elements which contributed to their success. But there is no "right" way to accomplish a work of art. The problem is to accomplish it in the most direct and economical way, economical of the time and spirit of the artist and economical of his resources. Involving a team or group to achieve the end is a difficult job of communication and administration.

Although I have expressed grave doubts about the industrial design approach to artistry in glass, there have been notable exceptions. I have come to know Sybren Valkema, presently associate director of the Gerit Rietvelt Academie of Amsterdam, and through him the designers at Leerdam. Valkema was a designer there for many years and worked with men he himself had taught at the glass school in the Leerdam factory. He was kind enough to give me two sketches of pieces produced in 1953, one of which is reproduced here. His understanding of the process, the uniqueness of his relationship with the skilled workers of Leerdam, and the atmosphere created by the then director of design at Leerdam, Andries Copier, gave birth to a great number of "Unica," unique pieces. Originally a student of the glass school at Leerdam, and now a leading designer there, Willem Heesen has pushed farther in a recent body of work in formal sculptural directions.

SCULPTURAL WORKS BY WILLEM HEESEN.
(COURTESY OF N. V. KONINKLIJKE NEDERLANDSCHE
GLASFABRIEK "LEERDAM.")

Opposite:
VASE BY ERIK HÖGLUND, 1950s.
THE ENGRAVING ON THIS PIECE
WAS DONE BY HÖGLUND HIMSELF.
(COURTESY OF HARRY DENNIS, JR.)

The aim of the design school at the Orrefors factory in Sweden is to help the worker understand the artist's function. Nevertheless a certain style is so strongly identified with the name "Orrefors" that the individual designer has much less impact on total production there than he might elsewhere.

At Boda Glassbruk, however, the directors hired a young sculptor, Erik Hōglund, and gave him free rein to experiment for as long as five years before expecting a return from his production.

Hōglund's work ranged over a wide expanse of possibilities, beginning with fanciful engravings, many executed by himself, to furnace work similar to that of Erwin Eisch, to direct cast forms which were assembled for architectural use. By the time of my visit in 1962, 70 percent of the factory's production were somewhat toned-down versions of his early work. Hōglund's interest in forged steel has led the factory to add a department to produce these items as well. Seldom have I seen such confidence in an artist by factory management. I had never heard of an artist receiving a five-year grace period.

Hōglund's pioneering brought another young artist to Afors, a subsidiary of Boda, Bertil Vallien, who is also experimenting freely.

Yet, with all the freedom permitted at Leerdam and Boda, the artist-designers still have not been able to expand the opportunities for glass artists, which is essential to our goal. Though Hōglund and Vallien could produce pieces in glass, other artists all over Europe were stopped at the front gates of the glass plant.

The aim of education in the European technical schools is to produce the students needed to fill the jobs known to be open in any given year. At the School of Arts and Crafts in Göteborg, one of two in Sweden, Rector Kurt Eckholm told me that they accept only four students in glass, because that is all that they can place.

We could not place a single student in industry, but we take all we can. America seems not to plan its production of students or artists, but rather to consume all that are produced. We are concerned with trying to make it possible for those who wish to study, to study whatever they wish.

The American concept of the relationship between business, education, and the arts was concisely stated by Frank Stanton, president of the Columbia Broadcasting System, in an address before the Arts Council of Columbus, Ohio. He said:

...I am not sure that the arts are not ultimately the meeting ground where the liberal education and progressive business come together. The aim of a liberal education is to give significance and nourishment to the individual human life. It is the arts, especially, that remind men of their humanity and of the sustaining values of our culture. And so the first place to worry about American life losing its vital qualities of individualism is in the arts.

Maija Grotell, my teacher, said once how glad she was to have chosen pottery as her field, because after thirty years, she could still see fifty years' more work to do. I hope to have outlined a few years work for myself and others in this fantastic material, glass.

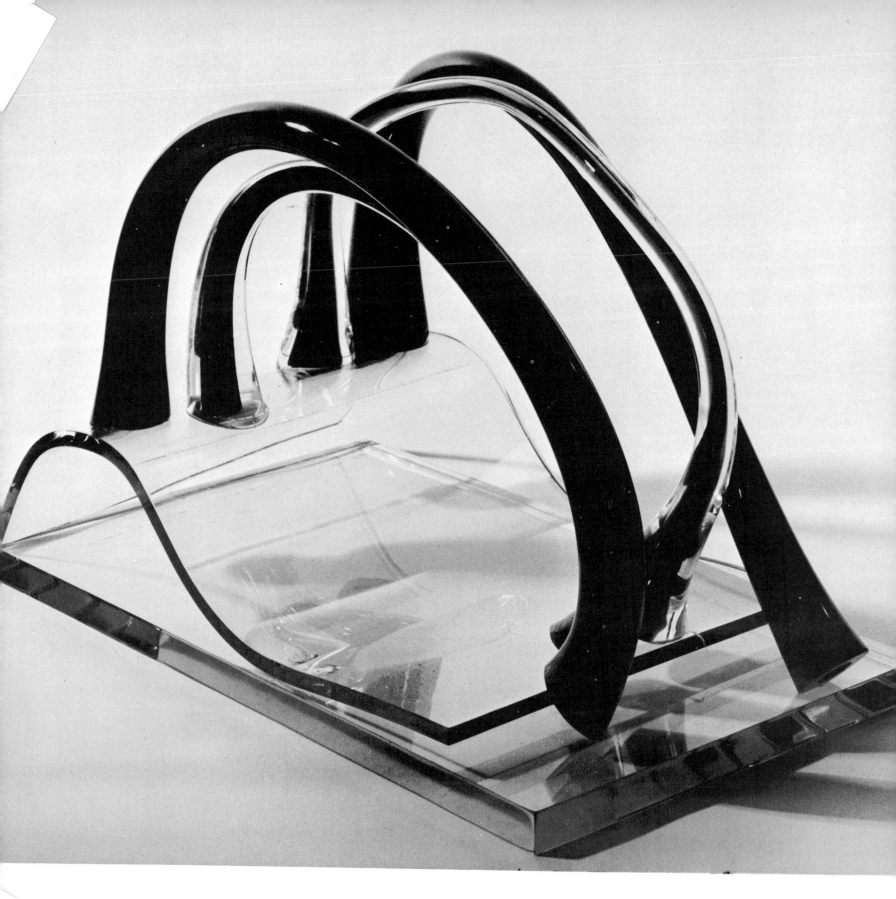

"FALLEN PURPLE,"
BENT PLATE AND MANGANESE TUBES AND RODS,
BY THE AUTHOR, 1970.

GLOSSARY

ANNEALING—Controlled cooling of glass in an oven in order to remove stress.
ANNEALING RANGE—The range of temperature at which an object can be annealed. The range varies according to the composition of the glass.
BATCH—The mixture of raw materials for glass before it is put into the furnace and melted.
BLISTER—A bubble in the glass.
BLOCKING—The shaping of a gather of glass in a block mold.
BLOWPIPE—The hollow tube of mild steel used for gathering and blowing glass.
BOROSILICATE—A heat-resistant, low-expansion glass; pyrex.
CAMEO GLASS—Several layers of different colored glasses, cut like a cameo.
CHECK—A surface crack.
CORDS—Glass inclusions of different compositions from surrounding glass. Cords are often the result of improper and insufficient mixing and melting.
CULLET—Glass which has been melted and cooled. Some cullet is produced commercially to be melted and worked by itself. Cullet may also be added to batch. The term also refers to any waste or leftover glass.
DEVITRIFICATION—The formation of crystals in glass after cooling.
FINE—To melt glass until it is free of bubbles. Some glasses are more difficult to fine than others.
FLAMEWORKING—The working of glass rods and tubes heated in a flame; also called lampworking.
FUMING—The coating of the surface of glass with a thin spray of metallic chloride, creating a wrinkled and iridescent surface.
GAFFER—The head of a glassblowing team in a factory.
GATHER—1. To get glass from the furnace onto the pipe or punty.
2. The molten glass on the pipe or punty before it is blown.
GLORY HOLE—A furnace or opening in a furnace used for reheating a piece of glass.
JACK—A versatile spring tool used to indent, stretch out, and form glass.
LAMPWORKING—See Flameworking.
LEHR—A continuous annealing oven in which pieces are moved along, mechanically or by hand, through the different stages and temperatures of annealing.
LIQUIDUS TEMPERATURE—The temperature at which, on cooling, crystals will start to form in devitrifying glass; conversely, when the glass is being reheated, the temperature at which the last crystals will dissolve.
MARVER—A slab of marble or steel used for rolling and chilling glass.
POLARISCOPE—A strain detector.
POT FURNACE—A furnace in which glass is melted in refractory containers, or pots.
PUNTY—A solid steel rod used for gathering glass and for attachment to the bottom of a blown piece so that the blowpipe may be struck off and the opening of the piece reheated and finished.
SEEDS—Small bubbles in glass.
SQUARE SHEARS—Shears with a square hole in the blades used for cutting a rod or a gob of glass.
STONES—Crystalline lumps in glass.
STRIKING—The appearance of color in glass after cooling and reheating.
TANK FURNACE—A furnace which contains the melted glass without pots.
YOKE—A Y-shaped support for the blowpipe.

BIBLIOGRAPHY

Abstracts. Eighth International Congress on Glass, 1968.
Altmann, J. P. *Das Neue Lehrbuch Der Glasätzerei.* Stuttgart: Verlag, A. W. Gentner, K. G., 1963.
Beard, Geoffrey. *Modern Glass.* London: Studio Vista Ltd., 1968.
Day, Ralph K. *Glass Research Methods.* Chicago: Industrial Publications, Inc., 1953.
Demoriane, Hélène. "The Master Who Blew Frozen Music." *Realités,* March 1968.
Hammesfahr, James E., and Stong, Clair L. *Creative Glass Blowing.* San Francisco: W. H. Freeman, 1968.
Haynes, E. Barrington. *Glass Through the Ages.* Middlesex: Penguin Books, 1948.
Hettes, Karel. *Old Venetian Glass.* Translated by Ota Vojtisek. London: Spring Books, 1960.
Koch, Robert. *Louis Comfort Tiffany, 1848-1933.* New York: Museum of Contemporary Crafts, 1958.
Labino, Dominick. *Visual Art in Glass.* Art Horizon Series. Dubuque: William C. Brown, 1968.
Lardner, Rev. Dionysius. *The Cabinet Cyclopaedia.* London: A. and R. Spottiswoode, 1832.
Lee, Ruth Webb. *Nineteenth Century Art Glass.* New York: M. Barrows, 1952.
Littleton, J. T., and Morey, G. W. *Electrical Properties of Glass.* London: John Wiley & Sons, 1933.
McKearin, Helen and George S. *Two Hundred Years of American Blown Glass.* New York: Crown Publishers, 1950.
Polack, Ada. *Modern Glass.* London: Faber and Faber, 1962.
Ruskin, John. *Handbook of Art Culture.* Edited by Rev. W. H. Platt. New York: John Wiley & Sons, 1877.
Scholes, S. R. *Modern Glass Practice.* Chicago: Industrial Publications, 1935.
Schrijver, Elka. *Glass and Crystal.* 2 vols. New York: Universe Books, 1964.
Schuler, Frederic. *Flameworking: Glassmaking for the Craftsman.* New York: Chilton Book, 1968.
Weyl, Woldermar. *Colored Glasses.* 2nd ed.; London: 1959.

The above bibliography contains a list of generally useful works on glass. More specialized works have been published by the major manufacturers of glass, including Corning, Steuben, and Orrefors. In addition, many museums, such as the Corning Museum of Glass, the Musée de Verre de Liège, the Toledo Museum of Art, the Cooper Union, and the American Crafts Council, have published extensive and useful works on glass. Articles on glassblowing have appeared in arts, crafts, scientific, and historical journals.

INDEX